Think Free
to Live Free

A political burnout's guide
to life, activism and everything

Think Free to Live Free

A political burnout's guide to life, activism and everything

by Claire Wolfe

Breakout Productions, Inc.
Port Townsend, Washington

Think Free to Live Free

A political burnout's guide to life, activism, and everything

© 2001 by Claire Wolfe

Cover Art by ☆

Published by:

Breakout Productions, Inc.
PO Box 1643
Port Townsend, WA 98368

Phone: 360-379-1965
Fax: 360-379-3794

ISBN 1-893626-45-8
Library of Congress Card Catalog Number 2001086291

Contents

To Tina — the brains of the outfit.

Introduction

We're bold, dedicated, courageous, idealistic, principled, and charged with vision. We're Politically Passionate People. We keep the world on track and keep its politicians on edge with our demands for truth and justice.

We are sometimes people on the fringe, people whose interests may lie far from the everyday. But our hearts are very much on center.

We may be anything from conventional campaigners to culture jammers or monkeywrenchers.

We're also burnt out, pissed off, head-banging and otherwise exhausted by the conflicts between our efforts and the response of the world. (Which tends to range from, "What's on the other channel?" to "F**k off and die, you [pick epithet of choice: wing-nut; bomb-throwing anarchist; eco-freak; black-helicopter whacko; dope fiend; reactionary pig].")

We often give our whole lives to losing causes. We do it because, like Martin Luther, we "can do no other."

But Jeez, guys, isn't there a way we can do it and still be a little easier on ourselves? Isn't there a way we can do it without burning our brains to a crisp with constant struggle and frustration? I think there is. After plunging several times into Politically Passionate Purgatory from causes failed or betrayed, or from poor personal choices, I think I'm finally beginning to develop perspective — and to know how to convey that perspective in a way that can be useful to others in the same fix.

What this book is and who it's for

This book is very simple. It's a workbook for *anyone* who cares about principles and causes — whether you be right, left, libertarian, anarchist, or a small-blue-alien from Beta Lyrae.

Specifically, it's for Politically Passionate People who are exhausted by their efforts, or who have the nagging feeling that their passions are, ironically, blighting their personal lives rather than enriching them.

I use the term "political" quite loosely. There is no better word, though there should be, to describe who we are. "Political" in our case doesn't necessarily imply voting or working on campaigns — not hardly! It does imply caring about the state of the world — justice against injustice, liberty against tyranny, the people against the powerful — and acting (rather than just wishing) for change. A Politically Passionate Person is an idealist in motion.

The book consists of nine short chapters. It's meant for you to use, scribble in, Post-it, annotate, argue with, chew on, and hopefully benefit from. Each chapter consists of about half text and half worksheets you can use to evaluate the current state of your life-in-crusade and where you'd like to head from here.

The aim is to help you be a more contented human being and (if you still wish to be) a more effective activist.

> ## You can also use this book if:
>
> - You're burnt out from your job and want change
> - You're burnt out from family troubles and need help envisioning ways out
> - You're burnt out from volunteer work and need renewal or recommitment
> - Even if you're burnt out from relentless pursuit of pleasure
>
> In other words, this book could be used by anybody who's weary of any current course of action and would like an organized way of 1) figuring out exactly what's wrong; and 2) deciding what to do about it. If your particular dilemma is not obviously connected to politics or philosophy, you might need to adapt the worksheets to other purposes. But the basic process is the same.

How does it work?

As the title implies, this book deals with both how you think and how you live. Though it is designed for activists, it is much more about life and attitudes than about activism.

Its fundamental premise is that, no matter how troubled the world may be, you have a choice in both how you feel and how you act in response to outrages and injustices. Also, that there are choices we can make that are both principled and personally fulfilling. (Unlike our frequent choices that are principled but self-defeating.)

This book offers no silver bullets, and no magical solutions. What it does offer is a way of thinking and training yourself out of your worst frustrations, your worst dead-end actions. While I offer no magic (sorry), you might nevertheless experience "aha!" moments that will enable you to leap over what looked like impassable attitudinal obstacles.

Who am I to write this book?

I once read a book about male-female relationships by a woman who stated, "I'm no social scientist. I'm just a person who's been known to throw up on the telephone receiver when her latest paramour announces that it's time to move on."[1]

That about sums it up here, too. I've been there, done that. Then been back there and done it again. (A slow learner, perhaps, but persistent.)

I hit the political road at age 12, trailing behind my yellow dog Democrat mother who herself was following her Socialist politician father. When I got the chance to touch an actual Kennedy, I didn't want to wash my hand for weeks.

---

[1] Sheila Gillooly, *Venus in Spurs*, Henry Holt and Company, 1996.

Later, I marched against the Vietnam War. But shortly thereafter, it became apparent that I was the only hippie carrying a copy of *Atlas Shrugged* down Haight Street. I have been, since developing my own political consciousness, a proud member of the lunatic libertarian anarchist fringe. The desire for individual freedom is, and always has been, at the core of my political consciousness.

Finally, though, it was the brief — and monumentally undeserved — trust I put in a crusading Republican politician that landed me on the path to writing this book for burnouts and disillusioned idealists. Her betrayal was, for me, the end of the conventionally political road.

After that, I started writing books such as *101 Things to Do 'Til the Revolution* and *Don't Shoot the Bastards (Yet)*, proposing alternatives to standard political action.

So I have not only been there and done that, but have been there and done that from every "wing" and no wing at all. And when I think about the gulf between my political cohorts and the allegedly "normal" world, I cannot discount the possibility that either we or they are also little blue aliens from Beta Lyrae in disguise. Activists are often that different from the rest of the world.

During my political journeys, I've hit more than one wall, flamed out and crashed several times, sunk repeatedly to the depths of despair, and on far too many occasions sworn I was going to give up all this crazy, hopeless crusading in favor of dedicating my life to studying reruns of *The Beverly Hillbillies*.

Yeah, right. When Jed Clampett stars in the next James Bond flick.

The reality is, we, the Politically Passionate may also be the Dramatically Doomed. We cannot turn off the caring, even at moments we most profoundly wish to stop feeling our own pain and all the world's pain, besides. But there are ways, and then there are ways, to do what we do.

At last, I have gotten some brains. Without caring one whit less about freedom and justice, I've put the political world in perspective. More important, I've learned to recognize some of my *own* unproductive, self-defeating reactions and to train myself to think and live more contentedly. I can tell you, it's one hell of a relief, even at the same time it sometimes takes one hell of a lot of effort.

I hope I can pass along some of that hard-won (and sometimes borrowed) wisdom in the following pages.

Chapter One
Burnouts of the World, Unite!
(You have nothing to lose but your pains)

Politically Passionate People:
Are you ... ?

- Burnt out?

- Accomplishing too little?

- Repeating the same actions even though they don't bring results?

- Angry or outraged too much of the time?

- Seeing your relationships suffer because of your Political Passions?

- Feeling as if nobody else cares?

- Carrying the weight of the world on your shoulders?

- Feeling responsible for healing every injustice?

- Wondering why it sometimes feels so wrong to be right?

- Sick of being treated like an outsider every time you speak your mind?

- Suffering through too many dark nights of the soul?

- Just plain tired of it all?

If so, this book is for you.

This book is for anybody, anywhere in the philosophical spectrum, who wants to combine effective activism with a fulfilling life.

This book makes no promises to cure the injustices of the world, and certainly doesn't promise to turn off your pain by turning you into a laid-back dude or dudette whose only ambition is to have the right brand of microbrew at your side while your team wins the Super Bowl.

What this book can do is help you put your political activities into perspective, build a more satisfying life, and be more effective in your political work.

Worksheets: The heart of the process

The heart of **Think Free to Live Free** is a series of self-evaluation worksheets. You can use these worksheets to sort out and analyze your activist skills, your personal values and your goals. They can also help you identify pitfalls you may have tumbled into — pitfalls that can be both tactical and emotional. Finally, they can help you build an action plan for the future.

It's possible that a few people will come out on the other side of this self-evaluation having discovered that they no longer want to be politically active in any form. Or that they want at least a hiatus from being Crusaders for Justice. More likely, you will emerge with a clearer idea of:

- Why you do what you do.

- What works.

- What doesn't.

- What you might like to do instead, and

- How you can be more effective and more at peace with whatever you do.

The evaluation requires only a few hours of your time but a great deal of your introspection. There is no scoring, no expert analysis, and there are no right or wrong answers. There is just the text, the raw material you put in, self-evaluation with the opportunity to gain insights into your heart and mind — and finally a set of action-planning worksheets. The more depth and honesty you put into the worksheets, the better result you will get. This may sometimes mean writing about mistakes, habits or personal motivations you'd just as soon not admit. However, nobody needs to see your words but you. If the goal is to feel better and do better in the long run, a few ohshit moments — or a few grumbles at yourself or the damn stupid author who's putting you through all this — shouldn't be too high a price to pay.

Here, specifically, is what we'll cover

Chapter Two: The raw material of an activist. In this brief chapter we'll look at the basics most of us have to work with — the relentless, idealistic, passionate, dare-all temperaments that characterize activists of all stripes (and the reason this book can equally serve left, right, libertarian, and small-blue-aliens). We'll take a look at what we can expect to do — and what we probably can't do — with our fundamental natures.

Chapter Three: Conflicts of interests. Here we'll start analyzing the commitments of our political lives and the more homespun things we value in our personal lives. Do our political goals and our personal goals match? Differ? Do they match — but throw us into conflict with our everyday world?

Chapter Four: How can it feel so wrong to be right? Here — in what may be the most difficult chapter for anyone contemplating personal change — we'll dig into the greatest difficulty many of us set for ourselves: the need to be righteous even when it makes us personally miserable. Still, there's hope even for the terminally just and self-justifying — without compromising what we believe.

Chapter Five: Are you having fun, banging your head against that wall? The ways in which we may fight the wrong battles — or the right battles for the wrong reasons.

Chapter Six: What are you best at? Leaving the most intense portions of the journey, we enter more comfortable territory. Here, we'll analyze our activist skills and experiences to see where we shine.

Chapter Seven: What do you *want* to do? Continuing the work of Chapter Six, and looking back on the worksheets of earlier chapters, we'll start putting it all together. Now that we've analyzed what we value and what we're good at, the question is: What do we want to do? — with our activism and other aspects of our lives.

Chapter Eight: Money, family, and other immovable objects. If you're suffering burnout, the causes and effects span many areas of your life. It's no surprise that job, relationships, or lifestyle may be contributing to your exhaustion. Consider that your burnout may be affecting your family relationships or your ability to earn a living. This chapter will point you toward some resources for getting around the more prominent Immovable Objects in your life.

Chapter Nine: Planning for action. Putting it all together and deciding where to go from here.

Finally, there's a **Resource Section** that lists books and Web sites where you'll find more guides to life change.

At the end of this process, you will not be a different person. The raw material and the Particular Passions of You will remain unchanged, but you may be more energized, more satisfied, more clear in your plans and more ready to go on to a life that fulfills you, as well as fulfilling your aspirations.

Chapter Two
The Raw Material of an Activist

A guerrilla leader was once asked what he would do if his side actually won — if his comrades took over the government of his country. He thought a minute, then responded, "Start fighting against the new regime."

For the Politically Passionate, that remark carries truth on several levels. First, it's a sure bet that any system will be corrupted — and therefore worth opposing — as soon as it's put into real-world action. People are imperfect and people in power are the worst of the lot. More important, for purposes of this book, the remark tells a truth about the nature of the speaker:

We who fight for what we believe are,
first and foremost, fighters.

In our political lives we're not the kind to say, "Well, nothing's perfect; I can live with *this* much injustice and not get too excited about it." In our personal lives, we're just not great at laying back, enjoying a toke or a smoke or a drink and letting the world take care of itself.

There's *always* injustice and we always get excited about it.

We may eventually give up on a cause because we're tired or defeated or have won a partial victory (as women's rights advocates did for decades after winning the long battle for suffrage). We may move from one issue to another as priorities shift. But we are always poised to plunge into the fray.

Unfortunately, this means we're not only perpetually at odds with the world, but perpetually at odds with ourselves, as well. We say we want peace, but our hearts are at war. We say we want freedom, but our minds remain bound to the battle with those who would steal our liberties.

"Well, of course," we protest. *"If we didn't fight for peace, the warriors would triumph. If we didn't fight perpetually to guard freedom, the tyrants would prevail."*

True enough. But (as we'll keep seeing elsewhere in the book) it's a kind of surface truth that keeps us from probing more deeply into our own hearts. By pointing a finger at our undeniable and very real adversaries, we're able to avoid looking at some of the ways we — by our nature or our acquired habits — exacerbate our own frustrations, fears, angers, and ineffectiveness in this lifelong philosophical battle of ours. *These* attitudes and behaviors — *our* attitudes and behaviors — are usually a major contributor to our own burnout.

We have minimal control over the state of the world, however much we wish and work to make it otherwise. Even powerful characters like Gandhi, Patrick Henry, Abbie Hoffman or Eleanor Roosevelt have limited impact in the long run (and not always the impact they set out to have, either). We have a lot more control over our *personal reactions* to the world. It is the goal of this book to help make those reactions (and our subsequent actions) less stressful, more productive and less wasteful of energy.

It may be a gradual process. It certainly involves commitment and dedication to self-change. As my friend Tina Terry, activist and teacher, puts it:

> X happens. It's a bad thing. You can't prevent it. But you have a smorgasbord of reactions ...okay, maybe a small salad bar of reactions ...you can choose from in that and subsequent moments.
>
> Each choice affects the next. By training yourself to respond in certain ways, you can modify your behavior so much over time that you actually modify your emotional reactions to feel less stress.
>
> It's kind of a bonsai process. Bonsai trees are clipped and trained and heavily modified by the gardener. This is kind of a self-bonsai process.
>
> Other analogies might be ballet training, or gymnastics, or karate. Think about how unnatural ballet is. The dancers turn out their feet, they make unnatural movements. When people begin training, they're clunky, they have to think very hard about everything. But when they finally reach unconscious competence,[1] they've trained their bodies to be in tune with their minds.

We can train ourselves, over time, to be less stressed by all the catastrophic goings on in the world — without numbing ourselves to injustice, without becoming callous, and without giving up or giving in. We can also get some quick results by eliminating from our lives some of the activities and conditions that cause our stress levels to go through the ceiling.

At all times, *this process is in your own hands.* No book author can "bonsai" you — and this particular book author cringes at the very notion. Whatever you do (or don't do) will be through your own decision, your own self-knowledge and your own efforts.

A certain amount of courage

It takes courage to look within and ask where we might be contributing to our own struggles. It takes honesty and an uncommon kind of determination to recognize and work on our own bad habits and attitudes. You may need to reach a certain age or a certain level of despair before you even consider that option. You may need to try a dozen courses of *action* before you turn inward to examine your *thinking*.

For some people it may take "hitting bottom" — as alcoholics and druggies sometimes must — before the realization comes: I need to change myself before I change the world. For others, it will be a very natural thing to do. And yet others may reject the whole idea, now and forever.

If this book isn't for you at this time in your life, how about giving it to a friend? You probably know someone who is burnt out or struggling for reasons that are murky (or reasons that may be obvious to you, but unclear to the other guy). Maybe this book could benefit that person.

"I yam what I yam and that's all what I yam"

Nevertheless, like everybody else, we activists are to some extent captives of our innate character, in thrall to our native temperaments. We have a certain raw material to work with. Just as you can't make supercomputers out of elephant dung, diamonds out of dandelion fluff or tofu out of beefsteak, there are certain things you can and can't make of yourself.

---

[1] The author/counselors Layne and Paul Cutright (http://www.enlightenedpartners.com) spell out four stages of skill development: unconscious incompetence; conscious incompetence; conscious competence; unconscious competence ("In the flow."). Tina credits work she has done with the Cutrights for many of her insights.

Obviously, we activists are all over the place in terms of personality, sex, sexual orientation, religious belief (or non-belief), economic status, tastes, styles of expression, etc., etc., etc. We're also (Does anybody really have to mention?) all over the place in viewpoints and goals. We drive each other crazy, and occasionally slaughter each other, over whether we are pro or anti-gun/drug/abortion/spending/military/prayer-in-schools/diversity/gay rights/government education/or the rights of dolphins, whales or huge, bloodsucking multi-national corporations.

But I'm willing to bet — in fact, I know — that beneath the issues and the stylistic differences, we are much more alike than different. And I'm not talking romantic stuff about us all being part of "the family of man" or "the oneness of Gaia." I'm talking about the temperamental drive that pushes unusual people like us to do what we do.

A "left wing" activist and a "right wing" activist, regardless of how much they might like to gut each other in a dark alley, have more in common with each other than they do with the booze-bellied dude lying over there in the hammock, listening to Garth Brooks.

That's why this book can be aimed at activists across the spectrum.

What are some of our common characteristics? While not every single one of the following will apply to every reader, here's a picture of what I believe we share.

We're devoted to knowing the truth. This doesn't mean you never let a lie pass your lily lips. Some activists are, in fact, championship liars. But we all tend to want to blast away veils of official secrecy, to demand accounts and accountability from politicians, to launch the spin into outer space so we can get at the down-to-earth reality. We don't like people in power hiding things from us. We hate plots and cabals, closed-door meetings and old boy networks.

We find ethical significance all around us. We value morality, ethics, or proper action. It's true even of we who see ourselves as pretty nihilistic or unusually open-minded. We make value judgments in places where most people don't even bother to glance.

We want to make a difference. It's why we're here.

We see potential for positive change. For some of us, this means visionary thinking, utopian dreams or actions to alter the nature of society. For others, it may mean no more than having a hope of *un*doing devastation or evil. If we didn't believe positive change was possible, we'd be over there with Mr. Beer Gut, taking a nap.

We have a tendency toward self-sacrifice. This shows up in the very fact that we're here, getting involved instead of hanging back. Some would say that's not self-sacrifice at all: "I'm doing this to build the kind of world *I* want to live in," but as a practical matter, we tend to sacrifice money, time, pleasures, and peace of mind to do what we do. Occasionally we put our lives or well-being at risk for our ideals.

We have very strong egos. We have to, to believe we can make a difference. We must, to endure living in a world that frequently tells us we're wrong-headed goofball extremist incredibly annoying wing-nuts.

We are concerned with social systems. We direct our energies toward reforming, revolutionizing, replacing, or sabotaging institutions — governments, societies, churches, businesses, and schools. Activists on the left may put the emphasis on *social*, while their compadres on the right may focus on *systems*. But as activists, even we libertarians (who see everything in terms of *individual* freedom) usually focus our political efforts on the institutions that can support — or destroy — what we most care about.

We have a strong work ethic. If not in our vocations or our home lives, at least in our activism.

We are empathetic. Unlike a certain snake-souled former president, many of us truly do feel others' pain — be it flood victims in Bangladesh, beleaguered taxpayers, inner-city mothers, or the family of a child shot dead by DEA agents in a botched raid.

We value action, not just words.

We worry about society falling apart. Or man's inhumanity to man. Or moral decay. Or the destruction of nature. In other words, we tend to see sweeping danger (and sweeping ethical implications) beyond every individual cause or issue.

We want to be of service. For some, this may mean direct, recognized service to humanity. For others, it may simply mean knowing in our hearts that the world is a better place because we were here.

We are driven by principles. Though some of us may be very pragmatic in action, we're always aware of the values that underlie both our actions and our goals.

You and I may otherwise be so different we couldn't find a word to say to each other if we were thrown together in a crowded room. But I'm as certain as I can be that every reader of this book shares at least 10 of those 13 traits.

Want to know more about temperament?

If you'd like to know more about your own temperament, or gain insight into temperament types in general, check out the books and Websites listed in the Resources section.

I've included URLs of free online temperament inventories — from a full-scale, 70-question test by psychologist David Keirsey to a four-question mini-test. Both of these use the Myers-Briggs classifications, which divide people into four main types and 16 subtypes.

While giving only an imperfect measure, these inventories and accompanying articles can provide an interesting glimpse of your nature and, perhaps even more important, offer sound advice on how to love, persuade, oppose, and put up with people of very different types.

Here's a guess: At least nine out of 10 readers of this book fall either into the "Idealist" or "Guardian" temperament type, as defined by Myers-Briggs.[2]

---

[2] Because I can hear a few readers asking already: I test as INTJ — Rational type, Mastermind subtype. I must have been having an Ayn Rand moment; I believe I'm actually closer to INFJ — Idealist type, Counselor subtype.

Why does all this matter?

It matters because *you* are the material you have to work with — your temperament, character, body, personality, skills, values, inclinations, and limitations.

I'm a huge believer in the ability to create personal change. Still, if you are already beat from head-banging, you can save yourself some effort (and a lot of money on self-help books) by knowing and accepting the raw material that is you — even some material you wish you didn't have.

For instance, if you tend to fall into periodic depressions and deep discouragement, it's likely that no book and no plan of life change (sans mood-altering drugs) is going to turn you into an ever-cheerful soul.

If you have workaholic tendencies, you might discover that no matter how much you wish for rest, you will invariably throw yourself into activity — even if the activity you took up was play.

If you're a worrier, you're probably going to go right on worrying to *some* extent, no matter how many gurus you consult about the problem.

No book can promise to cure all your ills.

That said, however:

- You *can* change all kinds of learned behaviors.

- You can *modify* even your most inborn tendencies.

- You can develop *techniques* for moderating any of your personal difficulties.

- And of course you can change thousands of things about your life circumstances — friends, job, activities, location — to make your external life better fit your interior needs.

For instance, someone who falls easily into discouraged states can learn to avoid circumstances that knock her down, or can teach herself little mantras and methods for getting through the hard times. A workaholic …well, that's usually cured by old age or early death. But you can also figure out what's compelling you to push so hard. Force yourself to take time out until it feels natural, practice meditation, or — after considerable examination of conscience — you can tell your critics to screw off, that you happen to *like* being a workaholic, you think everybody else is a lazy jerk, and if they don't approve of you they can hang out with someone else.

If you're a worrier, you may go on worrying; but you can learn to recognize it in yourself and say, "Oh, there I go again." It won't stop you from waking up at 3:00 a.m., filled with dread. But it might help you to go back to sleep and to go on with life. You can also use other coping techniques, from making lists of the things you need to tend to, to deep-breathing exercises.

I have a friend who has a sometimes frantic desire to fix other friends' lives. She may never lose that trait or the urge underlying it. But she's taught herself how to behave differently. One technique she uses is to make agreements with her close pals that, when one of them says lightly and affectionately, "Now, you know how you are, Romy," that's a sign that it's time for her to take a deep breath and stop pushing. Her temperament hasn't changed, but something as simple as that phrase — spoken with love, trust, and by friendly agreement — alters her awareness and defuses what could become an uncomfortable situation for all. (Since much of our stress derives from interactions with other people, enlisting others to help us function more effectively can be a good thing.)

It's often difficult to know — until you've lived a long time — what you can change in your life and what you can't. Or what you can change, but only at great cost.

I was once very inarticulate. I despaired of ever being able to sound intelligent in public. Each year I'd make a resolution: "Learn to be more articulate." Each year I'd be as fumble-tongued as ever. But finally, my own power of suggestion reached me and I discovered, to my surprise, that I could get up in front of just about anybody and say just about anything. (Some things I'd be better off *not* saying, unfortunately.) The first time I gave a three-minute speech opposing a government plan, I rehearsed it for five terrified days — but I got the only standing ovation of the evening. Today no one knows I was ever so shy, but what they also don't know is that exercising this hard-learned skill by going to a party or having a conversation with strangers is still the most difficult thing I ever do. I'd rather eat spinach with ice cream on top. My fundamentally introverted nature rebels. But I can do it.

Identity of an Outsider

A lot of us are distressed to think that average people (whoever those might be) dismiss us as fringe-oids and relegate our passions to the junk heap of life. Certainly, if your aim is to get something done, it's not encouraging when the media casually dismisses you as "an extremist," or when acquaintances start screaming when you mention drug decriminalization, anarchism, the right to own a bazooka, or your advocacy of state-sanctioned lesbian polygamy.

However, a lot of us (perhaps even all of us, at some time) get off on the image of ourselves as The Outsider. There's romantic appeal in being the outcast, the saint, the caped crusader, the pariah or the visionary too noble to survive society's banalities. (Colin Wilson, who coined the term, has written a whole series of books on The Outsider. The books are fascinating; the first and best known is listed in Resources.)

There's nothing wrong with this. Without Outsiders the world would be a very dull and much more repressive place. Without Outsiders, the world would be without most of *us*, as a matter of fact.

I mention it here primarily as a reality check. If you identify with The Outsider persona, recognize that fact and take it into consideration when dealing with the Real World. In those moments when you're feeling utterly whipped because you Don't Fit In and the World Won't Listen to You, remember that you also get something positive from not fitting. Remember that this image can lift you up, as well as get you down. Remember especially that your feeling is "your stuff" as much as it's "their doing." Remember that Outsiders are often recognized (post mortem) as the ones who spotted a truth before anyone else.

The same thing applies to people who love being in conflict. If you actually enjoy the fray or the heated debate, then Know Thyself — and resist the temptation to feel like a martyr when you get what you secretly want — a fight.

The long and short of it

- A lot of our despair and burnout comes from within, even when we have plenty of good reason to blame our political opponents.

- If you're burnt out, you need to change — not only what you're doing, but how you're thinking about it.

- We have the power to modify our reactions and to alter our habits and our activist activities.

- Change is more likely to come from self-knowledge, self-training and time than from guru-style miracles. Nevertheless, plenty of techniques are available to help.

- We have certain raw material to work with, and though we can accomplish all kinds of change, we can't alter our fundamental nature.

- That said, we can use the raw material that is us to become more fulfilled individuals and more effective activists.

Now, time to start looking at the stuff we are made of. In the following three worksheets, we'll list some of our own traits and start asking which ones drive us and which occasionally get in our way.

Worksheet One: Your temperament

In this worksheet, list as many of your own temperament traits as possible. It may take some time to remember a lot of them, but you can always come back to this table as you read and recall other things that are Very You.

Some of the traits listed earlier in this chapter might apply. Others (just to get you started) could include: optimistic, organized, outgoing, introverted, judgmental, perceptive, intuitive, natural leader, strong, pessimistic, tenacious, clear-headed, moral, unified in body and mind, independent, rational, innovative, creative, spontaneous, helpful, devoted, highly structured, warm, keeper of traditions, persistent, noble-hearted, good humored, stubborn, etc.

You can also get help with this worksheet by going to those Web-based temperament inventories listed in the Resource section. The Keirsey site, in particular, lists volumes of temperament traits.

1. If you know your Myers-Briggs temperament type, enter it here:	
Note a dozen or more of your most outstanding temperament traits.	

Worksheet Two: Traits that drive me to action

2. Of all the traits in Worksheet One, which are the ones that most drive you to political action? (List as many as you can think of and include a sentence or two to describe how they motivate you.)

Think Free to Live Free

18

Worksheet Three: Temperamental pitfalls

Both our most positive traits and our negatives may contribute to our burnout. For example, your passion for truth can drive you half-mad in an atmosphere of secrets and lies. Your native ability to work unstintingly may leave you exhausted and resentful of people who do less. Your impatience may make it impossible for you to stay the course. Your extreme and dogged patience may leave you baffled by co-workers who, not having your virtue, seem flighty and unreliable. Your desire for justice may lead to disillusionment in an impure world. Your drive for dominance may alienate those you rely on.

Think about your most outstanding traits, and note how they may thwart you, as well as how they drive you.

3. If you already know that some of your temperament traits contribute to your burnout (even if they are otherwise positive characteristics), list those traits here and write a sentence or two about how each affects you.

NOTES: Use this page to make note of anything that struck you while working in this chapter. In particular:

- Any insights into your heart, mind or present circumstances

- Any feelings that came up (particularly any uncomfortable ones)

- Any ideas for things you might like to have, do or be in your future

Chapter Three
Conflicts of Interests

One of the biggest reasons Politically Passionate People burn out (or at least spend half their time feeling as wired as a mosquito on a bug zapper) is that we can't live according to our values. That is, our political values don't mesh with the values of our lives. Or our political actions (which presumably follow from our values) interfere with the way we would like to live.

Let me give some examples of what I mean by values.

Political values might include a commitment to: Helping impoverished farmers; protecting gun rights; decriminalizing heroin; saving whales; preserving the Constitution; building communities; smashing the state; fighting zoning restrictions; saving free speech on the Internet; jamming corporate culture; opposing war; opposing taxation; ending racism. The list could be nearly endless — as could your choices of actions in those causes.

Life values might include a desire for: Solitude; time with family; physical challenges; avoiding BoBo Scum;[1] prosperity; security; simple, mechanical work; life in the country; fun-fun-fun; intellectual challenges; wide-ranging friendships; aesthetics; independence; public recognition; peace of mind, and so on.

When those values clash — when your life doesn't harmonize with your political beliefs or your political actions — you get all kinds of heart-and-soul sickness. You also get burnout.

When I'm talking about value clashes, I'm not talking about hypocrisy (though political hypocrites certainly abound, from the left-wing anarcho-strange-o who skillfully manipulates the media to declare that all media should be abolished to the Christian rightist who freely uses his Social-Security-Number-of-the-Beast while decreeing that the number signifies allegiance to the Antichrist). Hypocrites, bless their lucky little hearts, rarely burn out. They're so complacent that their pathetic little souls can't burn any better than wet toilet paper.

No. Real clashes and real burnout are the specialty of purists. We're idealists. We who eternally Aspire to Greater Things.

When I talk about clashes, I'm talking about those times — which for people like us is *most* times — when the realities of life prevent us from living by what we really care about. This can take a number of forms.

1. **A simple, practical problem of what's real vs. what you desire.** You want to go live in a yurt and open a sanctuary for wounded birds, but you're chained to your corporate cubicle by a pile of Visa cards and three aloof offspring who don't talk to you except to say "Nike" or "PlayStation2" or "tuition to Harvard."

---

[1] Now that all the Noxious Yuppie Scum have reached middle age and gone quietly into that good health spa, we have the equally unsavory Bourgeois Bohemians. Alec Baldwin comes to mind.

2. **A problem of your ideals being beyond your abilities to live up to.** You love all of mankind, but think most specific human beings are worthless jerks. You believe in freedom for the theoretical All, but happen to prefer ordering friends and family members around.

3. **The sad fact that the real world isn't set up for people like us.** The more you try to live your values, the more the world comes down on you, and that's what this chapter is really about.

Some instances of problems:

I just mentioned the hypocrite who decries the Social Security number but uses it incessantly. However, I've known people in the opposite spot: they've tried to do without SSNs — or at least to limit the number to its original purpose as a retirement plan account tracker. These people come from across the spectrum — libertarians who reject any government's authority to number them, Christian rightists opposing the SSN on religious grounds and civil-liberty left-wingers who fear an omnipotent Big Brother state. All are operating on their highest values.

Instead of being rewarded for their devotion to principle, these people find themselves marginalized. They struggle to get a job, finance a house, buy health insurance, get a credit card, purchase stocks, open a bank account — in some cases they can't even rent a video or get a library card. There they sit, falling into poverty while the nation prospers, having to fight to do ordinary activities their neighbors take for granted. Worse yet, for their sacrifices their acquaintances often see them as wackos, not brave defenders of All That Is Right And Good.

This also leads into a fourth way in which our values clash. This one is actually a subset of number three:

4. **When adherence to a deeply held philosophical value robs you of the opportunity to live a cherished life value.** For instance, when you desire prosperity but your principled stance keeps you poor. Or when your spiritual path lies through entheogenic drugs[2] — but that same path leads you to that barbarously unspiritual place, prison. Or when your greatest life value is to spend time with your family, but you feel compelled to give most of your non-work time to your beliefs.

Of course, principles — if you sincerely hold them — are worth some degree of suffering. But *what* degree? Under what circumstances? For how long? In how hopeless a cause? When should *political* principles take precedence over personal ones and when is it time to turn the tables? These eventually become looming questions.

Even if you have good philosophical answers, you can still be pretty miserable where the proverbial rubber meets that hard asphalt road.

If you're Politically Passionate, you can run into exhausting dilemmas anywhere, and they can take many forms.

- Hate buying products made with slave labor? Just try making sure no part of anything you buy comes from an objectionable source. It's an endless struggle.

- Believe that what you put into your own body is your own business? Explain it to the warden.

---

[2] "En·theo·gen [god within; god- or spirit-facilitating] a psychoactive sacramental; a plant or chemical substance taken to occasion primary religious experience. Example: peyote cactus as used in the Native American Church." See the Council on Spiritual Practices http://www.csp.org/ for more info.

- Believe in private property rights? Try telling that to the tax man, the zoning commission or the EPAcrat inquiring into why you filled that large puddle (aka wetland) in your driveway.

- Object to the harvesting of national forests? Rainforests? You could spend a lifetime diligently trying to avoid using products from these sources and in the end merely be very, very tired.

- Vegetarians don't have it quite as hard in our society as they once did. But vegans — who attempt to forego animal products in all forms —struggle every day to do things as simple as buying shoes or finding foods made without animal bits (in a world where even a harmless-looking bowl of Jell-O is actually a lump of animal-derived goo).

- Believe in your personal right to bear arms? Don't walk past a school. Or a church that holds Sunday school classes. Don't go to New York City. Or Chicago. Or Canada. You could get yourself busted.

So it goes. Those are all ways in which the real world conspires to thwart idealism. You may be able to do the things you care about, but rarely without constant niggling work and often not without enormous risk. You ask yourself, why should I struggle so hard to have the life I want — when what I want should, in the best of all worlds, be so simple and so harmless? And why do the people who don't care seem to have it so much easier than I?

Nevertheless, reality goes on demanding that you compromise your ideals if you want to function even halfway normally.

So what's wrong with compromise?

What's the big deal about that, some would ask? Even radicals know in theory that life requires compromise. In fact, we may be sweetly ready to compromise in a thousand circumstances. We'll compromise with our mate about which movie to see or with our co-workers about whether to have pizza or a veggie tray at the office party. We may even compromise with coalition members on political tactics. We just don't compromise with anybody when it comes to things that really, deeply matter. That's a big part of the reason we're in this burnt-out, head-banging fix, and that's also why we're often ineffective at achieving political goals.

Unfortunately, there's *always* a "can't win" aspect for those of us who care about something more than what's on TV or whether or not we'll get laid tonight.

I'm *not* going to suggest that you start compromising — that you become a gradualist if at heart you're a radical to the bone — that you ever go against what you hold dear. No way do I think you should move into the middle of the road and lie down on the yellow line. I do suggest that the better we understand our priorities, the better able we are to balance them or to make decisions about where to yield and where to hold fast.

Take, for instance, that man above whose highest life value is his family, but who devotes more time to political causes. He needs to decide which of his two conflicting values truly comes first — and how to act on that decision. He needs to know in his own mind what is right for him to do, and he needs to bring family members in on the decision, as well. It's painfully confusing to a partner or child to hear the conflicted message, "You're the most important thing in the world to me and really, I mean it, I'll get around to you one of these days."

On the other hand, once the man is clear in his own mind — *even if his decision is that they come second* — if he can explain that what he's doing is for their sake, or if he can bring them in on the decision, or make it clear that there's going to be a time limit to his political activities, or that no matter what happens, certain days will always be set aside for family, family members just might understand.

The following personal inventories can help you sort out exactly where your values clash or where your oh-so-consistent values bring you into a clash with the world. Even if you already have a pretty good idea of your priorities and feel you're acting consistently and making healthy decisions, this is an opportunity to start evaluating in a systematic way. If you already know where you are now, this is an opportunity to starting figuring where you might want to go from here. We'll use some of this information in later chapters.

As with everything else in this book, there's no scoring, no right or wrong answers. Just life.

When you *need* to be in conflict

Conflict is inherent in the lives of Politically Passionate People. Some of us, as we saw in Chapter Two, frankly get off on being The Outsider or the opponent. That's fine — as long as we recognize and acknowledge that trait in ourselves and understand how it affects our relationships and our encounters with Them, that world full of adversaries.

Some of us would prefer not to be in conflict, but are philosophically unable to make conflict-reducing choices — like those Christian SSN resisters who believe they must choose between God and government. Like anti-war activists who believe they would be complicit and responsible if they sat still and allowed war material to roll through their town.

In cases like these, you may simply have to find ways of living with the clash between you and mundane realities. Your best choice, if you wish to minimize the harmful impact of conflict, might be to make changes in *other* aspects of your life — buy and sell in the underground economy to reduce SSN conflicts, have a mutual help network to bail you out of jail, set aside one little corner where politics is never allowed to intrude — whatever lifestyle change or mitigation technique works best for your predicament.

Worksheet Four: Political values, actions and their consequences

In this worksheet, start by listing one of your major political values. On the next line, list the most recent action (or actions) that you performed as a result of that value. On the third line, note in as much detail as you can the consequences that resulted from your action.

In listing consequences, focus on the impact your political action had on *your personal life*. That is, how it affected your finances, time, family, emotions, friendships, health, etc. Include both the negative and the positive. You can also list *political* outcomes (certainly success or failure, since progress or regress affects your personal life, as well), but focus on the personal side.

Then repeat those same three steps for any other political values and recent actions. Use notebook paper if you need more room or want to list more value-action-consequence sets.

Here's a sample of what your results might look like:

Sample only:

1. My political value is: Legalizing hemp as a means of saving the forests and calling attention to the destructiveness of banning useful substances.

2. Because of it I recently performed these actions: Publicly distributed small, potted (non-THC) hemp plants at a demonstration; gave interviews to the media.

3. My actions had these consequences: Got arrested on public nuisance charges, but was released on $500 bail; might be facing more serious charges once they figure out whether I'm worth bothering with; when I got out of jail, my girlfriend and I had the hottest sex we've ever had. Life looked wonderful. My mother and father said they were embarrassed when they saw me on TV and I had to stave off an argument with them. I was tired as hell. Being in jail scared me. My boss said if I pulled a stunt like that one more time that I could kiss my job goodbye. Everybody else thought I was a hero. People I thought were hidebound old dinosaurs came up and said they'd always thought hemp should be legal. Having the cops close in on me was the scariest moment of my life; they went out of their way to be rough with me; but the whole experience was a rush. I felt I accomplished a lot. I liked myself. I felt good for standing up for what I believed in. I liked the public attention.

Now your turn. Don't worry if yours is somewhat more mundane (like: 1. Opposed new condo development, 2. Wrote letter to editor, and 3. Took forever to do it; writing and research were hard work; felt lousy when paper didn't run it; wondered why I bothered). Do as many different sets as you need to cover current values and recent actions:

| 4. |
| 1. My political value is: |
| 2. Because of it I recently performed these actions: |
| 3. My actions had these consequences: |
| 1. My political value is: |
| 2. Because of it I recently performed these actions: |
| 3. My actions had these consequences: |
| 1. My political value is: |
| 2. Because of it I recently performed these actions: |
| 3. My actions had these consequences: |

Worksheet Five: Life values

Make a list of the things you value for your daily living. Use the list at the top of this chapter (page 21) if you need help getting started. Try to write down at least 10 and as many more as you care to include.

Make your choices according to what you actually want, NOT what you think you ought to want, or what you think would make you look good to others.

You can write down things you already have in your life or things you genuinely want but don't yet have.

5. In my personal life I value:

Worksheet Six: Matching political values, activism and life

Now, take a look at the actions and consequences you listed in Worksheet Four. Then look at the life values you expressed in Worksheet Five. You will need to do some analysis of the information you listed under "consequences."

The question is: Do your political actions harmonize or clash with your life?

6. Referring to Worksheets Four and Five, list at least three ways in which your political values and subsequent actions harmonize with your life values.
1.
2.
3.

Referring to Worksheets Four and Five, list ways in which either 1) your political values and subsequent actions *clash* with the values of your real life, or 2) your attempt to live consistently with your values brings you into undesired conflict or compromise. List as many as apply. You may have zero. You may have 10 or more.

Worksheet Seven: Other impacts your political actions may have on your life

Even if you don't believe your political values conflict with your life values or life style, your political work may still be having an impact on your life in other negative ways. Ask yourself if some of these apply.

---

7. Are your political activities: Circle as many as apply

Leaving you too tired to enjoy other things?

Evoking paranoia?

Causing sleepless nights?

Taking too much time?

Arousing conflicts at home?

Affecting your job performance?

Discouraging you?

Throwing you in with people you don't like?

Destroying your concentration?

Causing you to waste time or spin wheels?

Keeping your temper high?

Requiring types of activities you don't enjoy or aren't good at?

Leading to headaches, backache, stomach upsets or other ills?

Costing you a lot of money?

Breaking your heart?

Other negatives? List them below:

Worksheet Eight: Closing the gaps

This next step calls for thinking about solutions, if conflicts between ideals and realities are dogging your life. You can either leave this worksheet until you've gone further in the book or go ahead and fill it out now, then compare these thoughts with those you have after making further progress.

Recognize in this section that the world — or your own temperamental realities — may never allow you to live in total internal harmony. Use this worksheet to consider ways to minimize the friction.

8. If there are significant gaps between your political actions and the way you prefer to live, OR between your political values and your life values, note at least one, and up to five, actions you could take to restore balance.
1.
2.
3.
4.
5.

NOTES: Use this page to make note of anything that struck you while working in this chapter. In particular:

- Any insights into your heart, mind or present circumstances
- Any feelings that came up (particularly any uncomfortable ones)
- Any ideas for things you might like to have, do or be in your future

Chapter Four
How Can It Feel So Wrong To Be Right?

A friend of mine defines insanity as doing the same thing repeatedly and expecting it to have different results. Yeah. How about when we also do things that are more complicated and labored than required to get a result?

This chapter is about the ways we drive ourselves crazy — particularly by being oh so righteously right.

Wait a minute! What can be wrong with being right? That's stupid! (So I hear some readers muttering — and so I would have muttered myself, as little as a year ago.) Being right is, by definition, the *right* thing to do.

A lotta things can be wrong with being right, mainly when being right occupies so much of your energy you forget to *have a life.* When you set things up so that being *right* keeps you from getting other things you want. When being *right* turns you into a twitchy mess of self-satisfied unhappiness.[1]

Like this guy I encountered not long ago. He may not have been political, but he sure was familiar:

I parked in a little neighborhood of beach houses and went for a walk. The spot where I left the truck looked like a dozen other tiny public shoreline accesses. It was a rare, fine day, so my dogs and I went for a leisurely stroll that took us far out of sight.

An hour later, as we wandered back into view, I noticed a figure standing in the lot. Thinking nothing of it, I dawdled along the shore, tossing sticks into the waves for the dogs to fetch.

It was a long time before I neared the truck. As I finally approached, I saw that the person was a 60ish man, and that he was hopping, twitching, spitting mad. At me. Clearly — and much to my surprise — he'd been waiting there solely to give me what for.

He informed me, shaking with indignation, that I'd parked on private property. *His* property. "You people always do this," he raged. "I get so tired of having to chase everyone out of here. Summer and winter, it's the same thing. Everybody treats this like a parking lot, no respect ..."

Indeed as I looked around the wide open area I could see plenty of tire tracks. It looked like the lot had gotten, and was continuing to get, plenty of use. There were no keep out signs, no fences, no chain across the entry, no warnings about trespassing. Just the open parking lot next to the beach, with a well-worn, inviting path leading onto the sand. I'll bet that land is getting plenty of public use to this day.

A single trip to the hardware store for a pair of $2.00 private property signs would have ameliorated the man's problem, and a chain across the entry would have ended it altogether.

Somehow, that man got more satisfaction from standing there twitching himself into a nervous frenzy — and being totally *right* about us damn trespassers — than he would have by marking his land private, then sitting back and enjoying life on the beach.

---

[1] Not to mention, of course, being *right* when you're actually totally *wrong.*

> *Discontent by itself does not invariably create a desire for change. Other factors have to be present before discontent turns into disaffection. One of these is a sense of power.*
>
> *Those who are awed by their surroundings do not think of change, no matter how miserable their condition. ...We counteract a deep feeling of insecurity by making of our existence a fixed routine.*
>
> *— Eric Hoffer*

Us, too

If we're honest, we've also got to face the fact that we've *been* that kind of person. At some time. In some way. Maybe we don't make such a petty, public display of stupid (in)action coupled with righteous reaction, but in fact, we Politically Passionate are often exceptionally good at being right. Right up to the point of pointless self-righteousness. Right up to the point of setting things up so we *get* to experience snits and lathers and frets and rages *that we don't really need to suffer* — just like old Mr. X did.

It's true that we often don't have it within our power to fix our situations, as that old grouch did. If you're *right* about hating a war that Your President loves, you can froth and protest all day and maybe that's all you can do. If you're *right* about a philosophical dispute with the taxbooted thugs, you can argue your position — but your position is going to remain face down on the rec room carpet while the SWAT team holds an MP-5 machine gun to your puppy dog's head.

A lot of us have the habit of getting into positions where we can be righteously right and lather and foam and cuss — all for nothing — even when we could just as easily avoid the whole thing.

This wears us out, hinders our effectiveness, and exacerbates any tendencies we may have to feel that the world is out of control — that *they*, not we — control our fates.

The tyranny paradigm: A really *bad* example of being right

As I was finishing this book, a friend reminded me of something called "The Tyranny Paradigm." I don't know who originated the phrase or first described the syndrome, but it's a particularly tragic way of being "right."

It begins when a Politically Passionate Person seizes on the idea that some government — whether it be city hall or the FBI — is powerfully dangerous. So far so good; that's an increasingly merited assumption. Then the person begins to act in a way that attracts the attention of the very forces he opposes. He writes letters that his already nervous opponents perceive as "threatening." He becomes known for his "far out" views or erratic behavior. He makes a defiant show of flouting laws. He commits deeds that a quieter person could easily get away with. Because of who he is, his opponents become increasingly watchful and increasingly itchy — until they finally pounce, sometimes with outrageous overkill.

Thus they prove he was "right" all along. They really were tyrants.

Probably the most famous recent example of this was Randy Weaver, a very personable man who nevertheless attracted enmity like a magnet — and lost his wife, son and dog in the bloody culmination. The federal government was absolutely at fault at Ruby Ridge; but they'd never have noticed the isolated little Weaver family, if not for years of provocative behavior.

There are certainly times when any of us could choose a course of principled action that would place us in harm's way. The writer Peter McWilliams did this with his open defiance of drug prohibitions relating to medical marijuana and died as a result. Sometimes we *must* take a stand, no matter what the risk. Certainly we should all be freer than we are to live, speak and think as we wish without retribution.

However, there is a difference between choosing to take a stand and simply behaving so provocatively that your attitudes create a self-fulfilling prophecy.

My particular Stupid Ire Rouser used to be writing letters to congressthings. Not just writing, but actually expecting politicians to read, think about what I'd said, and respond thoughtfully. Perhaps even to change their minds! (I know, I know, it's embarrassing to admit.) Naturally I'd get a form letter in response — which usually thanked me for supporting their position on abortion rights for dolphins when I'd actually written to oppose their perfidious chicanery on lunar colony currency controls. Naturally I'd bitch for weeks about what contemptible (*!!@!&%!~@~_%($*s they were.

Well they were, they still are, and they forever will be. I was right. So what? I cringe when I think about it now. All that wasted time and energy.

Understand, my real problem wasn't that I wrote to congressthings. My real problem was doing the same thing over and over again with the same unrealistic hope of getting a different result. My problem was doing something that got my own undies in a bunch, my own guts in an uproar — for nothing.

Here's another example. This is something one of my political acquaintances shared with me when I told him about this chapter:

> I used to do that. I hate unreliable people, but when you work with volunteers, unfortunately you encounter a lot of them. People will say, "I'll be there at 6:00 to help paint signs," then they'll come wandering in at 7:30 and do nothing but shmooze and kibbitz. They'll promise to send a donation, then "forget," or promise they'll make copies of handouts for a rally, but then just don't get around to it. When you

point out that they let you down, let everybody down, let the whole cause down, they look at you as if you're completely neurotic and say something like, "Hey, it was *only* volunteer work."

I spent years coordinating volunteers in [Political Party X]. I spent a lot of time trying to instill a sense of responsibility in these people, motivate them, remind them how important their commitments were. *Maybe* I got about two cents worth of results out of that, but the main upshot was that I was always feeling self-righteous and *they* still couldn't be counted on. I was completely pissed. Here I was doing things right and they were screwing up, but *they* were somehow "winning." I felt lousy about myself and they got to feel nice and relaxed and laid back, because I cared and they didn't.

Eventually I realized that if I was going to continue working with volunteers, my attitude would have to change. I could stay perpetually pissed — for no purpose — or I could accept that I'd have to do things like call and remind certain people of every, single commitment. I didn't feel I should have to do that. I was *right* that people should have been more conscientious, but what good did it do to be right? The point was to calm down and do what it took to get the job done. Man, I hated doing that, but it worked.

Changing our minds

There's some weird streak of human nature that would rather be right and miserable than to simply *stop* doing an unproductive thing. I can tell you from bitter experience that Politically Passionate People are among the worst in that regard.

It's understandable in a way, because it can take so much effort and such a change of heart, getting from here to there.

- First, you have to figure out what's not working.

- Then you have to decide it's possible to change the situation.

- Then (this is the hard part) you have to decide that the "situation" you first need to change is your attitude.[2]

- Then you have all that ghastly work of figuring out how to change what you're doing, and what to do instead. You're often facing some heavy psychological artillery from yourself at this point, not to mention a human tendency to just-plain laziness, not to mention having to explore the unknown and come up with workable alternatives.

It's all about enough to make you give up. Quite often we do give up because:

It's so much easier to stay stuck

and blame others (even *correctly* blame them)

than it is to fix US.

The not-so-easy secret

Thinking free to live free requires something very difficult. We have to honestly look at the ways in which we might be standing on our own stubborn rightness, or our own bad attitudes, to the detriment of our work, our mission, our relationships and our own peace of mind.

This kind of rightness might be affecting us in every area of our lives. A sure sign of it is whenever we keep running up against angers or frustrations of the above hair-tearing nature — over and over and over again, at home, at work, at play, at school, as well as in political work. For instance, a woman who has

---

[2] The usual response — I know, I know! — is, "Why should *I* be the one to change, when that other puking jerkfaced cretinous lump of toad excrement is the one who's in the wrong?"

rotten relationships with men might "get off" in this uncomfortable way by thinking, "All men are clueless jerks" and expecting the worst of them. Someone who lurches from one awful job or another might get rightness from his conviction that "work sucks."

Maybe they're right. Most work does suck. Big time. From a romantic female perspective, male cluelessness can stick out like ...er, other male things. (Sorry guys, you're just fine in other ways.) But that's not the point. The point is — does repeating that conviction, and the experiences that go with it, serve your peace of mind? Does it move your life forward? Does it make you a more effective human being? A more effective activist? A more fulfilled soul?

If not, bag it. Go elsewhere. Go forward.

If we want to get out of the rut, we've got to say:

- Even if I'm 100 percent right, that's beside the point.

- The question would be, is this attitude contributing to my life satisfaction or my effectiveness?

- If it isn't, that particular mode of thinking has got to go.

It may take some effort to get there. But truly, the hardest part is making that initial decision to *change our thoughts, even though we are right.*

Note that I'm not saying anybody ought to quit caring about the causes or things they feel passion for. I am saying, to care in a more life-enhancing, productive way, a way that's less inclined to lead into burnouts, ruts and headaches.

I'm also not saying you ought to paste on a Pollyanna attitude when your own experiences tell you that things aren't so sunny. But you ain't gettin' nowhere by sucking yourself into a black hole of righteous resentment. (I *know.* Been there, done that.)

Know any whiners?

Do you know any whiners? Sure you do. The world is full of them. They're do-nothings who'll happily suck away your time and energy — grousing about what's wrong with the world but never lifting a finger or contributing a dime to fix things. (Gasp! That would mean taking *actual responsibility!*)

Do yourself a favor. Give 'em a copy of this book. They still might not *do* anything, but they'll probably shut up when you imply they should think about their own actions (or lack thereof). At least they'll know they can't waste *your* time any more.

Actually, there are millions of whiners.

What the heck: Just call 1-360-385-2230 for information on ordering multiple copies. Benefit yourself, benefit me, and tell those whiners to put up or shut up. Share this book.

Doing it

Now its time to analyze where we may be stuck in unproductive attitudes and how we can get out.

The following worksheets might take considerable thought. Try to fill them in when you have an hour or more of uninterrupted time. It might help to take some deep breaths, sit quietly and really consider the answers, rather than just jotting down the first thing that comes to mind.

As with all the self-analysis in this book, there's no scoring, no right or wrong answers. These are just tools for you to use as you work. You'll get the most out of them if you put your real concerns — and your real self-revelations, even the painful ones — into them.

If you are concerned about anyone else seeing what you write, you may prefer to write on sheets of paper, conceal them in a safe place, then discard them when you've completed the process outlined in this book. Just don't neglect writing things down. The very act of writing will help you to think clearly and to see connections between apparently unrelated things.

Worksheet Nine: Top ten crazy-makers

9. What five things most frustrate or annoy me in my personal or work life?
1.
2.
3.
4.
5.

What five things most frustrate or annoy me in my activism?
1.
2.
3.
4.
5.

Among all ten items above, which three have been the most consistently frustrating or troubling?
1.
2.
3.

Worksheet Ten: What goes around comes around

The following table asks you to analyze similarities between the three most troubling problems of your life.

Take your time filling it out. Be sure to examine several sides of each problem — emotional, financial, physical, etc. In addition to analyzing the objective nature of the things that consistently trouble you, take a look at your own role in these dilemmas. Be open with yourself even if it's uncomfortable. Are you reacting in similar ways to each situation? Is there some way in which these three different problems hit a single "hot button" for you? Have your actions brought you into similar conflicts in different areas of your life?

Here's a sample of how this part of your self-analysis might be filled in for someone whose three most frustrating problems are: 1) lack of money; 2) failed relationships with women; and 3) involvement with seemingly hopeless causes.

These three problems may seem unrelated — until you look at them more closely.

SAMPLE ONLY:

Are there any common elements between your three most troubling problems?

SAMPLE ONLY: All three problems make me feel discouraged about the future. All three make it hard to sleep at night. My parents always said I was a loser, and these things confirm it. Problems 1 and 2 happen in part because I give up on things too easily. Problem 1 happens because I'm so busy putting my energy into Problem 3. Jobs suck. Women suck. The world sucks. Maybe I have a need to see myself as a screwup. All three problems involve beating my head against a wall and getting nowhere. My stomach lurches when I think about any of these things; I don't have a clue about solving any of them. Women don't like guys who don't have money, or who are more interested in causes than in them, so 1 and 3 might help create 2. I'm a hopeless romantic and no real job, woman or state of the world ever seems to satisfy me. Bottom line? I want everything perfect and I quit when it looks like anything's even got a wart on it — jobs, women, whatever. I go for the big causes because I can picture big, impossible solutions, but I can't accept grubby, everyday effort that just results in some grubby, everyday compromise.

Now go for it ...

10. Are there any common elements between your three most troubling problems?

Worksheet Eleven: Changes of mind

Even if your most consistent frustrations, anger-rousers or terrible troublers have real, external causes, is it even theoretically possible that you could handle them better by changing your thinking about them? If so, what kind of *attitudinal* changes could you envision?

You don't have to *do* the change. You don't even have to *want* to do it. You don't even have to believe it's *possible* for you to do. Just imagine it.

Focus on changes in attitudes or ways of *thinking* about problems. We'll get to actions later.

11. I could handle these frustrations better if I ...
1.
2.
3
4.
5.
6.
7.
8.
9.
10.

Worksheet Twelve: Change in Action

Changes in attitude can lead naturally to changes in actions. Problems that seem insoluble when you're stuck in frustration can dissolve (or at least look a lot easier to tackle) when you think differently about them.

In the following table, write three possible actions you could take to solve those three most troubling problems you listed at the end of Worksheet Nine. Again, you don't have to *believe* in your solutions. At this point perhaps you don't believe solutions are possible, but you should at least do this as an exercise in creative thinking.

Two guidelines:

You don't necessarily have to be totally practical, (Sometimes impractical solutions work great for idealists.) **but try to remain within the realm of reality.** For example: "Stuff this job and become an itinerant artist" might be a workable answer, even if farfetched. "Nuke the office" is just silly. (Unless you own a nuke and are really *that* pissed off.) Do try to be practical when any practical option presents itself.

Choose solutions that you — with your personality, character, and abilities — could conceivably carry off, even if you don't presently have the means or the desire. Don't choose something that only a superhero or a very different individual could do. If, for instance, you are a quiet, bookish person and likely to remain so, don't propose training to become an Olympic weight-lifter or taking up a second career as a glamorous globe-hopping terrorist. If you are utterly devoted to family responsibilities, even if family matters are currently eating your guts out, you should not propose walking away from the spouse and kids — unless you really feel you might really be driven to do so.

Turn to the next page for the worksheet.

12. Now, take each of those three most troubling problems and list three possible actions for solving each of them. As you do this, think about the change in attitude that might be represented by any of these solutions.
Problem 1.
Solution A
Solution B
Solution C
Problem 2.
Solution A
Solution B
Solution C
Problem 3.
Solution A
Solution B
Solution C

NOTES: Use this page to make note of anything that struck you while working in this chapter. In particular:

- Any insights into your heart, mind or present circumstances

- Any feelings that came up (particularly any uncomfortable ones)

- Any ideas for things you might like to have, do or be in your future

Chapter Five
Are You Having Fun,
Banging Your Head Against That Wall?

You want to be free. You want peace, justice, peace of mind.

Obviously, outside factors prevent this. The whole Western world seems bent on becoming a corporate-governmental police state operated as a joint venture by Coca Cola, AOL-Time-Warner, the Dixie Mafia and the Bush-Gore-Ivy-League axis. Catastrophe looms.

You can hardly relax and be happy at a moment like this. So how come that Claire Wolfe person is spouting self-indulgent nonsense about *personal satisfaction* and *easing frustrations*? What does she think this is, time to watch soap operas and eat potato chips? Doesn't she realize we've got to hold the world together before it goes completely to hell?

Yes, she does. Well, *somebody's* got to hold it together,[1] perhaps.

I firmly believe you and I might do a better job of holding it together if we hold *ourselves* together and if — in that same process — we stopped and examined whether our actions on behalf of freedom are well-aimed and effective, or whether we are spinning our wheels.

To do that, we need to take a break, stop banging our heads against political issues for a bit — and do some searching for what's *inside* our heads (that is, what's behind our actions).

Taking a strategic break

In his superb tactical manual for activists, *Rules for Radicals,*[2] Saul Alinsky made this observation:

> Every revolutionary leader of consequence has had to undergo these withdrawals from the arena of action. Without such opportunities, he goes from one tactic and one action to another, but most of them are almost terminal tactics in themselves; he never has a chance to think through an overall synthesis, and he burns himself out. He becomes, in fact, nothing more than a temporary irritant. The prophets of the Old Testament and the New found their opportunity for synthesis by voluntarily removing themselves to the wilderness. It was after they emerged that they began propagandizing their philosophies. Often a revolutionary finds that he cannot voluntarily detach himself, since the pressure of events and action do not permit him that luxury; furthermore, a revolutionary or a man of action does not have the sedentary frame of mind that is part of the personality of a research scholar. He finds it very difficult to sit quietly and think. ...Even when provided with a voluntary situation of that kind he will react by trying to escape the job of thinking. ...He will do everything to avoid it.

---

[1] Though I suspect both the world and human freedom are both more durable *in the long run* than we sometimes believe they are.

[2] *Rules for Radicals: A pragmatic primer for realistic radicals* by Saul Alinsky, Vintage Books 1989, originally published in 1971. Somewhat dated now, but well worth a read.

Alinsky made these remarks while encouraging radicals to put themselves into situations that would land them in jail. A short term in jail, he reasoned, had many benefits for Politically Passionate People — one of which was enforced time to think.

Let's hope *jail* isn't necessary for most of us — especially since sentences are getting longer and conditions more Draconian in this "enlightened" twenty-first century. But a strategic break of some sort definitely is merited. This chapter aims to offer a kind of mini-break. It asks you to take a few hours or a few days to think about:

- What you're doing
- Whether it's effective
- Whether it's life enhancing
- Whether it's what you want to continue to do

What you're doing

No doubt some readers of this book are still in the thick of conventional political processes — doorbelling, leafleting, getting out the vote, contacting their congressbeast and, in their hearts, wanting to believe in The System. Others have probably swung to the other end of the spectrum — complete nihilism, "What, me give a crap? I'm just going to smash stuff," or, "I'm just going to Cosmoline the AR-15 and wait."

But there's one given about Politically Passionate People: We always remain Politically Passionate, even when we change strategy or tactics, even when we try to tell ourselves we just flat won't, can't, don't care any more.

Even when you're walking your dog or petting your cat or reading to the kid or making mad, passionate love to your partner, some part of you is still Aware. Some part of you still capital-C Cares about the world. Because it is your nature.

Even if you're standing still or retreating, you're still politically active. For example:

- Just as it is a political action to register voters at a shopping mall, it is also a political action to go into the underground economy because you object to supporting the state with your labor.

- Just as it is a political action to demonstrate outside a convention hall, it is also a political action to quit doing that and volunteer at a soup kitchen.

- Just as it is a political action to vote, it is also a political action to stop voting and urge friends not to vote.

- Just as it is a political action to petition on behalf of medical marijuana, it is also a political action to get off the streets and *grow* medical marijuana.

- Just as it is a political action to write your congressman advocating privacy protection, it is also a political action to monkeywrench the snoop systems by getting fake ID and establishing records under half a dozen names.

In fact, in these cases, the apparent "retreats" from political action are actually more *committed* political actions. And many of them have greater potential to wear us out or endanger us.

Burn out especially happens when we think we're doing something to get away from The System (like going underground) — then find ourselves, against our inclinations, feeling as involved as ever.

Whatever you are doing to achieve Truth, Justice, Freedom, or The American Way, you'll face the questions:

- Does this work to achieve my political aims?

- Does it work for me?

Is it achieving your aims?

Obviously, accomplishing aims is relative. For the Politically Passionate, with our far-flung idealistic goals, it rarely means a sweeping victory and may mean doing nothing more than holding the line or preventing losses.

After all, even holding the line can be better than losing, and you never know when the flow can shift. Some "hopeless causes" have suddenly become hopeful. Such a shift has happened recently with drug decriminalization and privacy. So yes, holding the line can be legitimate.

Whatever you are fighting for, and whatever your objective chances of victory, you need to know whether *your specific actions* are moving you toward the goal. Have you thought out what you do? Have you determined it's the most effective thing you personally *can* do? Are you personally effective *within* a particular political effort and (a separate but ultimately related issue) is the broader effort successful in what it's aiming to achieve?

Though no one can define what is "effective" for every action, or every circumstance, here are some typical ways you might measure:

- If your goal is something as straightforward as electing a candidate or promoting legislation, the obvious measure is: Did you win?

- However, if you're in it for the long haul, you might consider your work effective if you 1) gained name recognition and credibility for the candidate; 2) got enough votes to retain your party's ballot status; 3) got a bill out of committee; or 4) got more votes on the bill than you did in last year's legislative session. All are indicators of slow steady progress to the next stage.

- If you protested in the streets to halt globalization, you probably didn't halt globalization. But you might consider yourself effective if you 1) shut down the meeting; 2) got X-many column inches of print coverage or top position on the evening news; or 3) earned a favorable article in a magazine wherein recruits for your position might be drawn.

- If you are working on behalf of a group, you might ask, "Whether we won or lost a particular battle, did we increase membership?" "Whether we won or lost a particular battle, did we increase our funding?" "Did we gain credibility?" "Did we make valuable allies?" "Did we put vulnerable politicians on notice?"[3]

An evaluation of effectiveness can be complex. Take the real-world example of The Fully Informed Jury Association,[4] the brilliant work of Larry Dodge and hundreds, if not thousands, of activists. FIJA's aims were to nullify bad laws by letting jurors know they had the right to acquit a defendant if they believed the law itself was unfair. FIJA also had the aim of getting state laws on the books, confirming that historically accurate, but now oft-denied, position.

What happened?

- They built a solid core of informed activists from all corners of the political spectrum.

- They got their message across to jurors, even though it cost the arrest of a number of activists.

- They earned a lot of credible media coverage, carrying their message to millions of potential jurors.

- Just when it looked as if the message was going strong, prosecutors retaliated by *excluding* from juries anyone who even expressed knowledge of nullification, or even showed signs of independent thinking.

- Judges also took it upon themselves to nullify FIJA by giving hard-line instructions to juries. In one case a judge even removed a juror for refusing to vote guilty; in another a Colorado court brought charges against a nay-saying juror.

- Finally, FIJA has yet to get a single jury-nullification law enacted anywhere.

There is no doubt that FIJA has been an admirable, well-organized effort conducted by some of the damned finest people anywhere. There is no doubt its aims are noble and that its ideas could bring about a revolution (actually a counter-revolution against elitist control) in the justice system, but has FIJA been effective or not? Has it been outmaneuvered by cynical politicians? Has it had a quiet, unheralded effect in the jury boxes of the nation? Has it — by the very act of being stymied — been effective in uncovering a ruthless power-hunger within the court system? Or is it simply too early to tell?

You, as they don't say in modern American courtrooms, be the judge.

A couple of ways we screw up

On the road to effectiveness, there are a couple of detours we habitually take. They're worth noting here.

Screwup 1: Fighting reactively. One mistake people "on the fringes" often make is to fight *reactively.* Our causes are unpopular, or are under siege from well-financed, powerful organizations. *They* have the public podiums. *They* can afford the TV ads. *They* get the corporate or foundation funding. *They* hold the offices. *They* manipulate the opinion polls. *They* hold sway. *We* get the shaft. Therefore, everywhere we

---

[3] Thanks to Charles Curley of the Wyoming Arms Rights Coalition and to Delbert Gilbow of the North Olympic Peninsula Phone Tree for the items in this list.

[4] http://www.fija.org/ P.O. Box 59, Helmville, Montana 59843, Phone/Fax (406) 793-5550; FIJA also inspired creation of Justice Unlimited (http://www.justiceunlimited.org/), a South Dakota-based group working for an even greater degree of informed juror participation in trials.

turn, we encounter some new legislative threat, we learn of some new outrage being perpetrated, we hear some pompously idiotic or prejudicial statement against us.

Our first reaction is to squawk. To strike out. To strike back. To deal *right now* with *that* threat. But that simply doesn't work as a long-term strategy.

An example:

> My friend Tina is one of the truly Politically Passionate. When I first met her, she would often put aside everything else in her life (including money-earning and personal relationships) to take aim at rotten new legislative acts, stupid politician statements, and egregious media pronouncements. Letters, editorials and articles damn near flew off the ends of her fingers — and they were brilliant and savagely *correct.*

> Only thing is, her writings never reached the obtuse political figures at whom she aimed (though they did help establish Tina's reputation with her peers). Worse, had those political jackasses even been remotely aware of Tina's (re)actions, they might have been amused at their ability to control her. All they needed to do was speak, and Tina would jump. Though she always stuck with issues she was truly committed to, she was accomplishing little, disregarding her own long-term strategic goals, burning up her formidable energies and putting her own life at the disposal of her opponents.

> Tina, however, eventually realized she needed to wean herself from her reactive writing and now takes aim only when she feels she can do some good with her words.

It's true that we are often — usually! — in a position where we need to take *defensive action* against bigger, better funded, more mainstream rivals. However, that's not necessarily the same as merely reacting.

Defense can still be conducted strategically. A certain amount of "reactivity" will certainly be part of a defense strategy (just as Ginger, being the one swooping backwards around the floor, had to react to Fred within the choreography — the strategy and tactics — of their dances). But we lose effectiveness when we make mere *reaction* the centerpiece of what we do.

Even in a defensive fight, you need to figure:

- What you want to do with your energies and skills

- What you're best at doing with them

- How much time you should put into it

- What offenses you may need to ignore to conserve your energy

- How realistic your aims are

- When you're on the verge of overdoing it

- When the thing you're doing simply isn't working

- Or when it's working — but some other action might work better.

Even in a defensive fight, remember, you can also go on the offense. A perfect example of this is a gun-rights group called Citizens of America.[5] Under the leadership of Brian Puckett, they produced a series of gut-wrenching radio ads — women making desperate calls to 911 to the sound of intruders breaking in —

---

[5] http://www.citizensofamerica.org/ Citizens of America, 2118 Wilshire Blvd. # 447, Santa Monica, California 90403

politicians mouthing anti-gun speeches while surrounded by armed bodyguards — and, through volunteer efforts, got the spots on stations all over the country.

The gun-rights movement is struggling against negative media coverage, encroaching legislation and big-gun lawsuits. The struggle has been mainly a defensive action, but in the midst of it, there was room for the powerful offense conducted by COA.

Screwup 2: Repeating what doesn't work. Another error we often commit is to keep doing the same things over and over when they don't work. Remember Chapter Four? There we examined the way we get ourselves into those kinds of loops, emotionally, but we also do it *tactically*. We cling to some form of action, growing ever more tense at its failures, yet not knowing what else to do.

The process goes something like this:

If, say, you're used to marching on Washington

at the drop of a picket sign ...

but you've come to the conclusion nobody's watching, let alone listening

to your message, then ...

I'm going to quit this nonsense. It's expensive. It's time consuming. The media doesn't even cover us, but the CIA and FBI are probably out there making lists of who we are. Damnit, I'm never going to beg for attention again. But oh god ...Freedom and justice are slipping away every day. If you don't watch every minute, some new outrage will be slipped into law or some new country will be invaded. More people will starve, more will go to prison. Nobody seems to care! There's only a handful of us who understand what's going on. If we don't stand up and protest, nobody will. "The only thing necessary for the triumph of evil is for good men to do nothing." It doesn't matter if what I'm doing isn't working. The important thing is just to keep trying. To do something. They've just got to listen, eventually. They've just got to. They can't go on ignoring what's so self-evidently right! So ...

I'm packing my bags for Washington again.

Of course, it's often hard to know what really doesn't work at all and what might work if you just kept at it, or got enough people to join you, or if new facts were brought to the public's attention.

So this is a very personal thing. You have to decide not only whether a particular form of action works, but whether it works *for you*.

The elusive target

Another reason why our crusades may go awry: Sometimes we're so preoccupied with what we oppose that we totally lose sight of what we're for.

A prime example is the old anti-communists of the Cold War. Some hated communism so much that they were willing — often eager — to impose upon America a system of secret informants, mass roundups of dissidents,[6] loyalty oaths, guilt-by-association and domestic spy agencies — some of the very characteristics that made Communist societies so obnoxious. They would certainly have said that desperate measures were needed to "preserve freedom," but they had lost sight of what freedom entails.

Examples of similar breeds still abound — from conservatives who claim to want smaller government except when big government could serve their ends (federal anti-abortion enforcement, for instance) to liberals unable to see that monumental federal programs to help the poor mainly enrich bureaucrats while driving marginal working class people into poverty.[7]

I'm not talking about bald-faced hypocrisy, but about honest short-sightedness, or the law of unintended consequences, or just plain getting off track.

Whenever we claim one goal while spending our time on activities that, in reality, lead to entirely different results, we (not to mention the rest of the world) suffer. It's damn near impossible to tell when we're doing this — until it's too late. But it's worth taking a look at because it's a major stumbling block for us and the causes we advocate.

Is it life enhancing?

Tina, the friend above who no longer fires her verbal missiles at random, observes:

Sometimes we need the fight to give us an aliveness, a validation, a sense that we exist. But one has to hold it in a way that's healthy for oneself and the world. It's a life force like fire or water. It can be used for good or ill.

I've read that we are genetically programmed to move, physically, and if we don't we're unhealthy. I wonder, are some of us genetically programmed to fight?

Because we're impelled to do this, the only way we can remain healthy is to unhook from a kind of desperate — and arrogant — assumption: "If I don't fight the world won't be saved." This desperation tends to be a characteristic of people who want to make a difference.

The key to being more satisfied and effective is — lose the desperation. It's offputting to others and a pain to yourself. You've heard, "Don't try to teach a pig to sing. It's impossible and it irritates the pig." It's an old saying. But people are always trying to teach the pig to sing, anyway.

---

[6] Never executed, but the FBI did track the whereabouts of "suspected subversives" for years with plans to intern them all if the order was given.

[7] I'm sure my fellow libertarians and I are equally prone to gigantic blind spots about the policies we advocate. But as no government has ever actually *tried* anything we propose — "Oh, golly, yes! What a great idea. I think I'll just go and abolish myself right this minute!" — it seems a moot point.

Are you trying to teach the pig to sing? Are you butting your head against a stone wall? Are you reacting, rather than acting on your own volition? Are you constantly getting sidetracked? Are you performing repetitive actions with little result? Are you truly aiming at what you want, or only at obstacles standing between you and what you want? Are you ineffective or discontent without exactly knowing why?

Are you just plain miserable?

We who've chosen (or been impelled) to "get involved" have elected to put aside certain pleasures to do what we believe is right. That's fine. But we also need to recognize when a course is healthy for us, personally.

We need to make that decision completely aside from whether our actions are effective for the rest of the world, but the delicious irony is:

Once we're doing what's really right for us,

we'll almost certainly be more effective, as well.

There can be a lot of reasons we are in a discontented state with our own activities and why we might need to pause, reflect and change course:

- Sometimes we make political choices for reasons that don't ultimately suit us — because we feel social or familial pressure, for instance (even pressure from decades-old childhood experiences), or because we received an ingrained belief from a Sunday school teacher that we *should* do certain things, or because "everyone else is doing it." Because it'll score points with an employer, or a girlfriend. Something like that.

- Sometimes we made a choice and followed it as far as we could — and now discover we're plodding spiritlessly along a road to nowhere.

- Sometimes we have simply changed. Grown in a different direction, and our activism is now merely a dull and dutiful thing.

- Occasionally we've actually won.

- Occasionally we've been defeated so decisively there's no point in going on.

- Sometimes we still care down to our very bones — but have worn ourselves out with caring so much.

Because we are Perpetually Politically Passionate, if we tell ourselves we can never relax until the battle is won we're telling ourselves we're entitled to *no* relaxation, no letup, no break, ever. It's to say that the rest of the world can dance while we forever trudge like donkeys. It's to say that life for us must be purgatory. That just plain doesn't make sense — unless that is your consciously chosen form of masochism.

If Saul Alinsky is correct — and I'm quite sure he is — refusing to relax and retreat now and then is also to condemn ourselves to mediocrity, at best.

It's time to pause, to reflect, and as Alinksy suggests, to *synthesize.*

Is it what you still want to do?

After pausing to reflect, you may want to go on doing exactly what you do, or you may choose any other course, from bagging it completely and becoming a Buddhist monk to modifying your tactics slightly, to simply devoting a little less time to your particular Political Passion. If you're fortunate your pause may lead you to a renewed, holistic vision of what you need to do.

Essentially, this whole book is about making those choices.

Even if you're certain that your ends, means, and personal desires are in harmony, do the exercises below to confirm and concretize what you know about yourself and your activities. We will use the information in later chapters.

This chapter's set of exercises requires some honest, perhaps even brutal, introspection. Because everyone has personal blind spots, you might want to do one or two extra things with the inventory below:

1. Copy your finished self-evaluation from this chapter and show it to two or three friends. Pick people who know you well and who you can count on to be utterly honest with you. It might help to choose at least one person who doesn't share your political views. Ask them for their impressions of what you've written: Are your statements accurate descriptions of yourself? Are your statements complete descriptions of yourself in this area, or have you overlooked something? If so, what insights would your friends add?

Or

2. Photocopy the blank exercise forms and ask two or three friends to fill them out *as if they were you*. In other words, have them evaluate *your* goals and conflicts *as they perceive them*, while you also fill out the forms on your own behalf. Again, be sure to pick people you can count on to be totally honest with you, including one or two who don't agree with your viewpoint. Ask them to be as straightforward in their evaluation of you as possible (even if they think it's going to hurt). Between these various inventories, you should get a pretty good picture of your political self as it looks to you and others.

Worksheet Thirteen: "And it's 1, 2, 3, what are we fightin' for?"

In the next two worksheets, you may want to make photocopies and fill out different sheets if you are involved in multiple activities.

13. What is the major thing you're fighting for? And what are your major activities in that cause? Briefly describe.
Why are you involved in this cause?
Why do you choose these specific activities?
Do you feel you could somehow be doing better or be more satisfied if you changed something about your activities?

Worksheet Fourteen: Evaluating effectiveness

14. In the activities described in Worksheet Thirteen, what standard(s) would you use for judging their effectiveness?

Were the activities themselves successful by that standard? Explain why.

Was the work you personally did effective in helping meet that standard? Explain why.

Worksheet Fifteen: Specific recent activity

15. What were your five latest *specific* Politically Passionate activities? (E.g. Wrote a letter to a congress person, sabotaged a Nike factory, marched on city hall, made calls on a phone tree, blew up an IRS office, planted hemp on the lawn at city hall, etc.)[8]
1.
2.
3.
4.
5.
In *these* activities were you ... ? Circle the one that best applies

Mostly reacting to what an opponent was doing	Doing a roughly equal mix of both initiating action and reacting	Mostly initiating action in pursuit of my own long-term goals

I'll bet if your recent activities have been mostly reactive, you're feeling more tired and burnt out than your pal with the positive motivations.

---

[8] I'm only kidding about the illegal stuff. If you did it, DON'T WRITE IT DOWN.

Worksheet Sixteen: What moves you?

16. In your Political Passions are you sometimes motivated by ... ? (Check as many yeses or nos as apply.)	Yes	No
What your parents might think about your actions		
The fear that if you don't do it, nobody else will		
A desire for approval by those you work with		
A desire for gratitude from those you work for		
Fear of personal failure		
What teachers or other authority figures told you you *should* do		
A wish that others would do as much for you as you do for others		
A feeling that people are too helpless to take care of themselves		
A belief that people will screw up their own lives if laws or organizations don't protect them from themselves		
The feeling that you must do *more* for others than anyone does for you		
What your friends, relatives or neighbors might think of your actions		
Your ideal of what a moral person would do		
A sense that you're sinful or inadequate and need to overcome that or make amends for that		
An absolute compulsion to act, to do something *now*		
A memory of abuse or injustice committed against you as a child (or that you observed as a child)		
An enjoyment of making the opposition squirm		
Having others perceive you as an outsider or an unusual person (even if their perception is negative)		
Guilt because you have it so much better than many others		
Identification with hopeless causes		

Every one of us is going to have some of the motives above. But if you have more than five or six "yes" answers, or if you felt a twinge in your guts at *any* of the above statements, then you're probably being driven by motives other than your own healthy desires.

It doesn't really matter whether the twinge took the form of, "Oh god, yes, that's me!" or "Hell no, what a stupid thing to imagine!" If you had a strong emotional reaction to any of the above motivations, you ought to go back and ask *why* that particular thing hit you that particular way.

For instance, one very logical male friend who guinea-pigged this self-inventory reacted with instant scorn at the thought of being motivated by his parents' approval or disapproval. "They're both dead," he sniffed. "Anyway, I haven't cared what they thought since I left for college." But when we talked about it, it turned out my friend was powerfully motivated by a desire to please — or at least avoid the wrath of — his ever-judgmental father and his harpy mother. His logical soul simply disliked the idea of being motivated by dead folks.

This is not to say that there's anything inherently wrong with any of the above motivations. Some of you guys might really get off on making your opponents squirm. No big deal. There's a very cavemannish aspect to it. Others, women particularly, are going to spend a lifetime wanting to please mom, or to have friends perceive us as helpful and good. No problem there — as long as we know what we're up to and recognize how that particular drive affects what we do and how we feel about it.

Worksheet Seventeen: Anonymity in action

17. What if you had to do all your political work anonymously? If no one observed you, no one heard about you, no one knew that you were the person writing the letter, making the donation, delivering the food or organizing the march, would you … ? (Check as many yeses or nos as apply.)	**Yes**	**No**
Be more effective; make even more of a difference		
Be less motivated		
Quit doing it altogether		
Feel relieved — and quit working so hard at it		
Be disappointed — and quit working so hard at it		
Feel relieved — and go right on doing it		
Be disappointed — but go right on doing it		
Get off on the fantasy of being like Zorro or the Scarlet Pimpernel		
Be angry and feel it was unjust to receive no recognition		
Feel as though anonymity was morally better		
Feel safer, less of a target for your enemies		

Again, there's no absolute moral charge on a preference for anonymity or public recognition (unless, that is, you share the views of Jesus, who had definite opinions on the subject). Chances are, the more comfortable you feel with the idea of anonymity, the more likely you are to be doing what you do because it truly satisfies you. The more anonymity bugs you, the more likely it is you're motivated by factors other than your own true devotion to your cause.

Worksheet Eighteen: Answering the questions

18. Overall, does your activism enhance your life? If so, how? If not, why?

Overall, does your activism achieve its aims? If so, how? If not, why?

NOTES: Use this page to make note of anything that struck you while working in this chapter. In particular:

- Any insights into your heart, mind or present circumstances

- Any feelings that came up (particularly any uncomfortable ones)

- Any ideas for things you might like to have, do or be in your future

Chapter Six
What Are You Best At?

Now, we get into the more practical, hard-headed, easier parts of the book. You've already looked at what matters to you and where you might be setting emotional or strategic traps for yourself. Now it's time to look at your skills, experience, inclinations, and how they might contribute to your next Politically Passionate move.

Use the worksheets in this chapter if you:

- Are burnt out on your current activities, but aren't sure how you can best apply yourself to your present cause or any future issue.

- Are completely up in the air — don't know whether you want to continue your present activities or not.

- Know exactly what you want to do, but need help "selling" your skills to others (say, if you're running for leadership of an organization or hoping for a job with an activist group). These worksheets can help you recall and analyze your strong points, as well as organize information about yourself in preparation for making a powerful presentation.

- Are looking for a non-political job, and as part of that process want to promote the skills and experiences you've gained through political work. The worksheets can help you organize that information for your resumé or interview.

- Just want a reality check on what your strengths and experiences are. Or perhaps want a well-earned ego boost. Sometimes we discount what we've done and what we know *when we're not getting paid for it*. (Sad, but true.) Making a tally of things you've done, the skills you have, and the things you've learned from your activities can, all by itself, be tonic for a mild case of burnout.

Because this chapter has a fair number of worksheets, and because a personal skill inventory is pretty much self-explanatory, I'll just get out of the way now and let you at it.

Moving toward other kinds of change?

As I reviewed this book's manuscript prior to publication, I had to wonder how many readers — even dedicated, lifetime activists — would take the time this chapter requires to analyze their political skills and activities. It struck me that many would willingly conduct an extensive personal inventory where money and career were involved, but not to analyze their non-professional activities — no matter how huge a part such activities played in their lives.

For those whose activism is central enough that you'll take the time — go for it. However, these same worksheets could also apply to your career. With a slight change of wording, you could adapt them to analyze your employment skills and experiences. Just think "job skills" where I've written "political skills," and so on. Since burn out (from whatever source) often does involve a need to change vocation, that's as "legit" a use as any in a book about re-thinking life.

There's also the distinct possibility that you might get a job with an activist organization, think tank, lobbying group, political party or other employer for whom your political skills will be an asset. So:

- To use these worksheets to improve your satisfaction and effectiveness with political work *only*, use them as they're written.

- To use these worksheets for non-political career development, fill them out with information about past and present jobs, not political experiences.

- To use them to project your political experiences into potential employment, use them as they're written.

- To use them for multiple purposes, make copies and fill out one set for politics, one set for jobs, one set for religious work, one set for what you've learned as a parent, one set for hobbies ...anywhere you think you could benefit by analyzing your skills, experiences and knowledge of a subject

Worksheet Nineteen: What have you done?

From the time you first became politically active, what efforts have you been involved with? And what specific activities have you done within those broad efforts?

Here's an example of the kinds of things you might list and the way to break them down:

Sample only: **What political efforts have you been involved with?**	Sample only: **What specific activities have you done in those causes?**
Opposed Gulf War	• Organized letter-writing campaign among local groups • Investigated and distributed early reports of Gulf War Syndrome
Worked to end War on Drugs	• Wrote articles on behalf of Rene Boje legal defense • Petitioned to get medical marijuana initiative on ballot • Studied economic impact of legalizing hemp for use as an industrial fiber • Wrote articles and letters on benefits of hemp
Opposed indiscriminate electronic surveillance	• Learned enough about various software to guard my computer against casual electronic snooping; taught friends how to do the same • Researched and distributed alerts about companies and government agencies known to invade privacy • Publicized the problem when local police secretly installed video cameras on my city's downtown streets
... and so on ...	

Now your turn. List as many causes and activities as you can think of, even ones that seem minor. If you're an old veteran with many years of experience, go ahead and use several pages of a notepad to list your activities. (Alternatively, you could just list the activities of your last five years; but you risk leaving out something interesting and important for your future.)

19. What political efforts have you been involved with?	What specific activities have you done in those causes?

Worksheet Twenty: What skills did you develop?

Skill means, loosely, the ability to do something well. It may be an inborn talent, an acquired ability or a combination of the two. For instance, some people have a natural leadership ability that shows up in their earliest years. Others might be shy and awkward, but learn to assert themselves because they strongly want to or need to be successful. In either case, their leadership ability counts as a skill.

Other examples of skills might be: ability to apply logic, media manipulation, carpentry, persuasiveness, writing ability, fundraising savvy, research expertise, talent with numbers, diplomacy, acting talent, organizing ability, athletic prowess or strong public speaking.

Virtues like moral strength, determination or honor wouldn't normally be considered skills in this sense, and we have covered them earlier, in the values chapter. Try to avoid including values or abstractions here.

Now, looking at the activities in Worksheet Nineteen, make a list of the skills you acquired, used, developed or discovered in yourself while pursuing Political Passions. For instance, in studying and reporting on industrial uses of hemp, you might have used such skills as 1) superb Internet and library research, 2) organizing detailed information into a coherent form, and 3) writing persuasively (among others).

List the skills — even minor ones — in the worksheet below.

20. In this activity ...	I acquired these skills ...

Worksheet Twenty-one: In what area do your skills lie?

Psychologist John Holland developed a theory of vocational choices that lumps everyone's interests into one of six broad categories. His work is widely used for career guidance. It's noted for helping people understand the general areas where their personalities and interests fit. While Holland dealt with *interests*, not skills (and we will, too, in the next chapter), you could also gain from seeing which groupings your particular *skills* fall into.[1]

In this next step, take the skills you listed in Worksheet Twenty and place them in the category where they fit best. If you feel a skill belongs equally in two categories, go ahead and insert it in both.

(I want to stress that while I've borrowed Holland's classifications, this adaptation to skills, rather than interests, is solely my own, and any inadequacies in it are also mine.)

---

[1] It's perfectly possible to be in the awkward position of having skills that do not match your interests. This might come about if you've been forced into a career choice by demanding parents; if you've gotten involved in activities because of your friends' interests, not your own; or if you've simply changed over time.

21. Categorize your skills.

Take each skill listed in Worksheet Twenty and put it in the category where it best fits:

1. Realistic — Practical, concrete activities. Outdoor work or work relating to nature. Work with tools or machinery. Physical skills.

2. Investigative — Scientific or intellectual pursuit. Gathering information, uncovering new facts or theories, analyzing or interpreting data.

3. Artistic — Aesthetics. Art, music, drama, literature. Self-expression. Skills suited for unstructured, flexible environments.

4. Social — Skills for working with others to help, train or better them in some way. Group activities, shared responsibilities. Skills involving problem solving through discussion of feelings and interactions with others.

5. Enterprising — Skills for influencing, leading or managing others (particularly for the sake of organizational, governmental, or financial goals). Persuading others to your viewpoint.

6. Conventional — Skills requiring attention to detail or fine accuracy, such as office work or accounting. Skills for working within a large organization or a fixed chain of command.

In Worksheet Twenty-one, in which area did the largest number of your skills fall? (Circle one)

| Realistic | Investigative | Artistic |
| Social | Enterprising | Conventional |

The second largest? (Circle one)

| Realistic | Investigative | Artistic |
| Social | Enterprising | Conventional |

The third largest? (Circle one)

| Realistic | Investigative | Artistic |
| Social | Enterprising | Conventional |

Worksheet Twenty-two: Which skills do you most like to use? And why?

Look at the skills you've listed in the worksheets above. Pick the five you'd most like to use in pursuit of your Political Passions. List them, then explain in detail why you want to use them.

For example:

Sample only: **List your top five skills and the reasons you want or like to use them.**
1. Persuasive public speaking
Reasons to use: Influence many people at the same time; promote my reputation as a leader and as an expert; gain publicity for the issues I feel strongly about; influence legislation by making presentations at public hearings; personal satisfaction — I get a good feeling afterwards; personal challenge — It isn't easy, but each time I learn something new; meet new people and bring them into activism.
2. Organizing marches
Reasons to use: Influence many people; gain publicity for issues; develop own leadership skills; I enjoy "flamboyant" activities; I feel I'm meeting my civic responsibilities; I like being outdoors, seeing flags and picket signs waving in the air; I feel that marches are one of the most visible and potentially effective forms of public protest; I am committed to non-violent means of change.
… and so on …

Turn to the next page for the worksheet.

Your turn ...

22. List your top five skills and the reasons you want to use them.
1.
Reasons to use:
2.
Reasons to use:
3.
Reasons to use:
4.
Reasons to use:
5.
Reasons to use:

Worksheet Twenty-three: What do you know?

We've dealt with skills — the things you *do* well. But there's another aspect of your abilities that's just as important as what you can do. It's what you *know*. (And sometimes *who* you know, but that's a different story.)

Do you have special knowledge in some area that might help you in choosing your future course? Think hard about this. It could be knowledge that at first appears to be entirely outside of the political/philosophical realm, but that might have some unexpected application. For instance, an expertise on amphibian mating habits might be applicable to an environmental cause. An extensive mental catalog of local rock groups might help you organize a fundraising event. Your knowledge of computer graphics might help you forge identity papers for a fugitive on an underground railroad. An old-fashioned teacher's knowledge of grammar could help you rip a bad law or legal argument apart. (My friend Tina, to whom this book is dedicated, once appeared in court as an expert witness for the defense. Grammar was her expertise. By diagramming the sentences of a tax law, she was able to demonstrate that the law said nothing coherent and therefore that the defendant could not have obeyed it even if he'd tried.)

In this worksheet, list your areas of knowledge. Write down only those things in which you have more-than-usual knowledge. But where you have that kind of knowledge, write it down even if the subject seems too trivial or obscure for practical use.

Here's a sample:

Sample only: **List subjects on which you have a more-than-usual expertise. Include even trivial or obscure subjects, as you never know what you might be able to put to use.**
1. Conspiracy theories; I know every theory of every sort, going back before the Bavarian Illuminati of 1776.
2. I know the inner workings of several types of exotic weapons systems, as well as the recipe for gunpowder and various ways of improvising weapons to use homemade powder.
3. Rock groups of the Chicago area, past and present.
4. Calculus, trigonometry; I was a math whiz in school.
5. The history of utopian movements in nineteenth-century America.
6. Cooking, specifically barbecuing; I won the regional cookoff for pork ribs and chicken.

Your turn ...

---

23. List subjects on which you have a more-than-usual expertise. Include even trivial or obscure subjects, as you never know what you might be able to put to use.

Use another sheet of paper if you have more kinds of knowledge than can be listed here.

Worksheet Twenty-four: What are your greatest accomplishments? And why?

As we've already seen, when talking about Political Passions, the word "accomplishments" can be relative. It doesn't necessarily mean you set out to topple a corrupt congressman and succeeded, or that you aimed at ending a war and did so. Alas once again, for idealists like us, accomplishments are often much more limited — and may be pretty subjective as well.

An accomplishment, in these terms, may be something you started that spurred others on to even greater achievement. It could be something you did that helped you develop new skills. It could mean winning a partial victory where you didn't even believe that much was possible. It could be a deed that didn't accomplish a lot, in itself, but opened doors to new opportunity. It could mean something that helped people feel better about themselves. It could be an act of monkeywrenching or destruction that helped achieve a larger aim. It could be an anonymous act of kindness. It could be a victory over some negative aspect of yourself, as long as that victory made you wiser, more effective, or more useful to your cause.

But it should, in each case, be something that had a real-world impact, however small or localized. (In other words, please don't list, "I took a noble stand in a hopeless cause, and by damn, I felt righteous." We've already covered that sort of thing. Being noble and right is certainly Us All Over, but that's exactly the type of "accomplishment" that's burning us out. So you may hold it in your heart as an accomplishment if you wish. But as a practical matter, please don't list it here — unless it had an effect you can sincerely say you're satisfied with.)

Go back to Worksheet Twenty. Pick out the *five specific activities* you feel had the greatest impact. List them below and analyze why you feel these activities were successful.

An example:

Sample only:
List your five greatest accomplishments in political passion and the reasons you consider them successful.
1. Acted as regional coordinator of grassroots "Jones for Congress" campaign, 1994.
Reason it was successful: First-ever primary election in this state that was won on a write-in vote. The timing was right, and Jones was the right person. Voters were mad at Clinton-style policies and ready for rebellion, but until I convinced Jones to run, they had no interesting option. I played a part in an unprecedented effort to get supporters to the polls; superb use of media, which I helped coordinate. Worked with powerful, committed candidate who campaigned on issues of principle; no mud-slinging; won the general election. Pulled off a minor miracle.
2. Secretly coordinated "Boot Jones Out of Congress" campaign, 1998.
Reason it was successful: Drove lying legislator out of office. Made amends in the most effective way for having gotten the idea to put that backstabber into office in the first place. No mud-slinging; stuck to issues, told the truth about her votes, and the truth did the job. Wrote several influential, issue-oriented essays that evoked controversy but had the desired effect. Public was ready for her departure. Her support had always consisted of a strong minority and a lukewarm majority; I succeeded by joining with others to undermine her core support. She took the risk of announcing a bid for the Senate, instead of trying to hold on to what she had. I not only helped assure the failure of her Senate campaign, but crushed her political career so utterly she'll never rise again from that coffin containing her native soil.
… and so on …

Your turn ...

24. List your five greatest accomplishments in political passion and the reasons you consider them successful.
1.
Reason it was successful:
2.
Reason it was successful:
3.
Reason it was successful:
4.
Reason it was successful:
5.
Reason it was successful:

Worksheet Twenty-five: Summing up your skills

Review all the worksheets in this chapter. Write at least one paragraph, and as much more as you wish to write, analyzing, in your own terms, your political skills and accomplishments.

Make this more than just a rehash of the above material. Include personal observations, hopes, aspirations, ambitions, feelings *about* your skills or achievements. What do your skills mean to you? What are your political accomplishments worth to you?

25. Overall, my political skills ...

So much — for the moment — about what you are good at. An equally important question is what you *like* to do and want to do — in activism, life and the universe. That's the subject of Chapter Seven.

NOTES: Use this page to make note of anything that struck you while working in this chapter. In particular:

- Any insights into your heart, mind or present circumstances

- Any feelings that came up (particularly any uncomfortable ones)

- Any ideas for things you might like to have, do or be in your future

Chapter Seven
What Do You *Want* To Do?

This chapter is about deciding what you want to do. Not what you want to achieve on the world's stage, but deciding what activities and plans you want in your life from here until the next turning point. As with the rest of the book, this refers not just to your activist life, but to other aspects of your existence, as well.

At the beginning of Chapter Six, I commented that we'd entered the easier part of the book. Well, I lied. I didn't mean to lie, and in fact this chapter and Chapter Nine ought to be the most pleasurable of the lot. But sometimes knowing what we want is harder even than looking at where we might be screwing up.

1. First of all, it requires us to move out of our nice, comfortable inert psychological state. ("I can't accomplish anything, anyway, so why try?") Even when our state is sour, it often feels sweet to savor it, simply because it's ours.

2. Figuring out what we want also commits us to the concept of change and all the hard work and risk that might imply.

3. It requires us to enter that strange and dangerous territory between what we ideally want ("world peace, a billion bucks and a private island") and what we can realistically hope for (which may be more, or less, than we *think* we can realistically hope for — like a better marriage, a little more prosperity, an Audi, or a slightly less dishonest congressman).

4. It requires us to think "selfishly" — something most libertarians are comfortable with, but which tends to give a lot of other people fits (but which we all do *anyway*; it's just a matter of whether we take care of our own needs consciously and healthily or covertly and twistedly).

5. Finally, it's often hard to *know* what we want — especially when we're burnt out and dispirited. At such times it's hard to find our next path forward and may be hard even to exert the energy to look.

Still, we can get past all this, even if we don't exactly know where we'll end up in the end.

Points 1 and 2 …well, if you've read this far, you're probably already there. So let's skip those and go straight to Point 3.

What you want vs. what you can attain

How do you know how high (or how low) to set your expectations?

I knew a guy a few years back — call him Mighty Mitty — who was convinced that someday the world was going to recognize his vast, Gandhian, Christlike, transcendental wisdom. He would be internationally beloved. He would transform the consciousness of the planet. And besides that, he'd rake in the Big Bucks.

How was he going to make these millions? Well, that remained somewhat vague. One Christmas, I gave him a little book of aphorisms — at that moment soaring up the bestseller lists and turning its previously unknown author into an internationally beloved millionaire-guru. Mitty barely turned the pages. "I could do better than this," he sniffed.

"Ok, why don't you?"

"I don't have a word processor."

So I bought him a word processor. (Like I said, I can be a little slow on the uptake.) Then I waited while he used it to write little notes to friends and a newsletter for a local business.

"But what about the book?"

"I've realized people aren't evolved enough to receive my message."

I wrote the word processor off as a bad investment, got the heck out of there — and have not exactly been waiting with bated breath for this guru wannabe to show up on the *New York Times* bestseller list, the Forbes 400 or the pope's list of candidates for beatification.

The interesting thing about Mighty Mitty wasn't his ability to deceive himself (or me). It wasn't even the grandiosity of his expectations. It was that he was so busy envisioning what he *might* do, given the perfect, shining circumstances, that he literally didn't bother to *do* anything. He never held a job. He certainly never even sat down to outline a book. He got by narrowly on charity tasks given to him by friends. And he waited — in poverty and resentment — for the world to recognize his Greatness.

Now, hopefully none of you good readers is as fatuous as he or as naïve as I. Aside from a Jupiter-sized ego, the biggest aspect of Mighty Mitty's Perpetual Poverty Problem was one most of us have to a lesser degree: He couldn't envision a realistic goal, and therefore couldn't take effective steps (or in his case, *any* steps) to approach what he *claimed* to want.

When I talk about "envisioning" I'm not talking some airy thing about positive thinking or affirmations or whatever the current motivational buzz is. I'm just talking about picturing what we might be able to do, today or tomorrow, that would bring us more satisfaction, personal or political, than we have now.

The problem can be the same with those of us who want world peace or worldwide justice, or perfection in human relationships, or any vast, idealistic goal. But it can also limit the success of people who have no goals or goals that are far too modest.

A common example of the inability to envision something realistically achievable is the person who absolutely detests his job — but stays and stays and stays, or the person who hates her marriage — but never bothers to fix it or leave it. Both end up settling for crumbs.

Partly those forms of inertia arise from that little quirk we covered in Chapter Four — that weird all-too-human characteristic that makes us prefer to bitch than fix things. But partly they arise, too, from inability (or unwillingness) to envision something better, or inability to feel entitled to something better, or to make the effort to go for something better, or to take the risk of leaving the familiar for the unfamiliar.

The result is similar, whether we envision too little or too much;

we fail to take effective steps toward what we could achieve.

If we are Mightily grandiose or too willing to settle for crumbs — either one — we're likely to end up settling for crumbs. And it's the same in both personal life and activism — which by now are inextricably mixed.

What we need is some *realistic* idea of what we want to do. Not only what we want to achieve, but what we want to *do* toward achieving it. This *may* mean envisioning a long-term goal, but for a burn out it may simply mean envisioning, and moving toward, some realistic emotional resting place.

What's realistic? Ah, there's the rub. For *somebody* out there, it might be perfectly realistic to hope to be an international millionaire guru or the king of Silicon Valley or the leader of the next revolution or to spend life in a perpetual orgy of sensation without ever having to pay the proverbial piper. Hey, it happens. To somebody, sometime. (Though it seldom strikes by sheer cosmic power, as Mighty Mitty seemed to believe.)

For most of us, though, it might just be a matter of saying, "I could quit and go into business for myself." Perhaps, "I absolutely hate this feeling that I have to run the organization or it'll die. I'm going to be a soldier in this fight, not a general." Maybe "I need more time with my dog." Even "I want to work with people who are different than the ones around me."

To make the goal realistic — neither too high nor too low — requires a lot of self-knowing, a fair amount of trust in yourself, and usually a lot of trial and error. No book can instill any of these things, but I hope this one has been (and continues to be) helpful with self-understanding and giving you other tools you need to help you move ahead.

Getting what you want by expecting more

I once sat in on a meeting of a state gun-rights coalition where the *entire discussion* focused on "what the other side might let us have." Every time anyone would make a proposal that actually offered any hope of *gaining* something (instead of merely minimizing losses), the others in the room would vote it down, refusing to add it to the group's agenda, because, "Oh, no, the legislature will never let us have that."

Well, any good union negotiator would have turned over in his grave (even if, as in Jimmy Hoffa's case, the grave is probably a concrete foundation block in a sports stadium somewhere). Can you imagine going into *any* negotiation having already reduced your bargaining position to *what you think your opponent might deign to grant you?*

You don't ask for what you can get; you scare your opponents to death with your high demands — then get them to "compromise" for more than you expected to gain in the first place.

A bit of the same principle can apply to going for what you want in your life. Don't "demand" so much of yourself that no mortal could achieve it. But don't "give in" and settle for crumbs before you've even tried, either. Set a goal that's maybe slightly scary, slightly out of reach, then aim for it.

You may fall a little short. You may achieve the goal. Or you may exceed it. But in any case you will 1) have gained a reality check on your abilities and limitations, and 2) made progress toward whatever it is you want.

Even if it turns out to be a kind of *negative* progress — finding out you don't really want what you set out to achieve, or finding out your abilities aren't up to the task, you will have gained because you'll have learned something that will help you with your *next* move in life.

Looking out for ourselves

On to point four. This section is especially for people who fear that doing what they want might be "selfish," or wasteful. Therefore, this next little bit isn't for all readers. However, it's interesting that even a lot of us who feel perfectly okay, intellectually, with the idea of taking care of ourselves, still may have psychological prohibitions and inhibitions about taking the time to pay attention to ourselves and go for what we really want.

You can skip this section if you never feel guilty or uncomfortable about tending to your own needs, but it's short. You might as well stick around, even if you don't believe you need it.

Did your mother ever tell you, "It is better to give than receive?" Mine did. Boy, did she ever. Mothers aren't the only ones who broadcast this message; we're universally supposed to believe it.

Still, it's pretty obvious that, presented with the choice between giving and receiving, most people's *actions* show that they'd damn well (and rather sensibly) choose to receive any day, no matter how many pious platitudes they mouth. Really, while there are certainly unhealthy manifestations of the desire to receive, there's nothing wrong with the impulse itself. It's simply human nature.

The thing is, whether you give or receive, whether you bust your buns trying to save the children, or the dolphins, or the Constitution, or the last Victorian building on Main Street, you're still pursuing your own self interest. Even if you choose to sacrifice yourself completely, as long as you make the choice (or take actions that are bound to lead to martyrdom), you're still pursuing your own self interest.

Mother Teresa of Calcutta was pursuing her self interest. Gandhi was pursuing his self interest. They decided to do what was important *to them*.[1] That their choice, their interest, also benefited others may have been a great plus. That's certainly what those two set out to do. But it was their own interest that drove them to do it, nonetheless.

There's nothing wrong with that. You were born a self. Your needs are as valid as anybody else's. (Not *more* valid. But no less.) And when you choose a course from your *enlightened* self interest (a great phrase from Ayn Rand), you're probably doing what's best for you *and* for the rest of the world — because you are acting with clarity, integrity and without inner conflict. You are more healthy, more capable of healthy interactions with others, more capable of producing healthy results, and more capable of raising the world's general level of inner peace. In another great phrase, this one from Joseph Campbell, "follow your bliss."

Okay, okay, the guys in the back of the room are taunting, "That makes it okay to murder and rob if you happen to feel like it!" Oh, groan. No it doesn't. Because that's denying other people the opportunity to pursue *their* self interest. "BUT," the little voices continue to object, "you're encouraging people to be selfish, self-centered pigs who don't care about others."

No way. A person who clearly understands that he (like everyone else) has legitimate needs and desires is likely to behave more kindly and more healthily than someone who feels he has to illicitly "grab" his own pleasures at others' expense (typical behavior of the self-twisted person we call "selfish").

---

[1] Even though Mother T. would surely have said it was what *God* wanted. Even if you grant her that, then she still made the decision that doing *God's* will was in her own best interest. We Protestants often don't realize that *a desire to achieve personal sanctity* is a perfectly legitimate reason to enter a religious order. And Mother T. clearly had much more than that going for her.

The real bottom line, for purposes of being both satisfied and effective, is to recognize what your own interests are and pursue them in the most conscious, loving way you can — not with all the quibbles we usually feel (we women especially, alas) about being "selfish," and not with all the emotional twists and pits that come from unconscious self-denial.

Yes, there are selfish s**ts in the world, and we all have our moments. The truth is we activist sorts are usually so into giving and sacrificing it's pathetic, and sometimes we do it in a way that's unhealthy for us and for others.

Classic example: I had dinner at a friend's house with a woman who volunteered in a poverty program. She absolutely knocked herself out "helping" people. Yet through that entire dinner conversation, it was apparent that she considered *all* people, not just those in the program, to be helpless, stupid, incapable of making practical decisions about their own lives, and in desperate, constant need of supervision by people such as herself. Yes, she was knocking herself out — but only as a kind of *noblesse oblige*. "So many inferiors — so few superiors to oversee them!" Her view of the world was arrogant, distorted, sick and sickening; I doubt very much that she was able to do any long-term good for her clients while projecting the message that they were a bunch of helpless sub-humans who couldn't be trusted to blow their own noses without her guidance.

No doubt this woman considered herself to be selfless, and heroically helpful. She was, in fact, a walking pathogen — delivering a poisonous kind of "help," indeed.

The point is: she was pursuing her own self interest, like everyone else does. However, because she couldn't be "selfish" enough to stop and examine her own motives and desires, she ended up performing the truly much more selfish act of using vulnerable people to serve her (unexamined) need to feel superior. Had she been able to back off for a while, do the "selfish" thing of figuring out "what's up with me and where does my real satisfaction lie?" she might have been able to serve both herself and others a lot better.

I'm going a bit far afield here, with this highly psychological example. The bottom line truth is that when we're doing one thing when at heart we're really wanting or feeling something else, our dissatisfaction may erupt in all kinds of gross, destructive ways: from whining and backstabbing to giving ourselves psychosomatic illnesses to performing actions that (like that woman's) have the opposite effect from what we claim to desire. When we know our own desires, we can act with more clarity and less covert conflict.

Be selfish. Figure out what you really want. Even if you can't go for it just yet, you'll live and act more clearly for the knowing.

This is not about becoming a selfish pig. It's not even about encouraging you to pursue a life of personal pleasure. It may well be that your greatest interest *does* lie in helping or sacrificing or leading others into dangerous battle.

This section is simply about knowing what you *really* want to do.

There is nothing wrong with having, or being, a self.

The self denied will find a twisted way out and produce twisted effects.

Know thyself.

And, oh yeah, follow thine own *enlightened* bliss.

What do you really want?

Point five, the final point on our table of difficulties, is another hard one. Knowing what you really want means sorting out the truths of your own heart, mind, and temperament from all the cultural and intellectual layers that might have been imposed upon them. It also means having a recognition of what's realistic *for you* — what someone with *your* beliefs, desires, assets and experience can go for.

It means taking what you've learned from experience and recognizing what's valuable and what's dross. It means more of that dreaded self-examination — but not as onerous as some you might have done. This step should be liberating and can be fun.

So how about we just get on with it?

Worksheet Twenty-six: Exercising your "I want" muscles

This worksheet is to get your brain limbered up, in case you are really stuck, or in case you really have an inner prohibition against wanting what you want. It should also be productive for anybody by helping you identify the things you most want to do (and most don't want to put up with).

Very simply, in the following three tables, write:

1. Ten things you're sick of

2. Ten things you enjoy

3. Ten things you want to do

These things can be in your work, your hobbies, your family, your intellectual or emotional life, your activism — any part of your life.

Don't think too hard about them. Just write what comes to mind. You can go back to earlier worksheets for inspiration if you wish, but don't feel these 10 have to be "the most important 10" irritations, pleasures or desires of your life. Just see what comes up. Possibly, something will arise that you were unaware mattered to you. Maybe something will come up and will assume an importance you didn't previously recognize.

If you really want to get into free association and write more than 10 in any category, just grab your notebook and go.

NOTE: You may notice yourself writing down some of the same issues you brought up in worksheets in Chapter Three or Chapter Four. Don't worry about that. If different issues come up, you're exploring more aspects of your burnout and your future. If *similar* issues come up, you're telling yourself all the more clearly that *those* are the ones that you need to work on. Either approach is fine.

Turn to the next page for the worksheet.

26. In this table, write 10 things you are sick of.
I am sick of
I am sick of
I am sick of
I am sick of
I am sick of
I am sick of
I am sick of
I am sick of
I am sick of
I am sick of

In this table, write 10 things you enjoy.
I enjoy
I enjoy
I enjoy
I enjoy
I enjoy
I enjoy
I enjoy
I enjoy
I enjoy
I enjoy

In this table, write 10 things you want to do.
I want to do
I want to do
I want to do
I want to do
I want to do
I want to do
I want to do
I want to do
I want to do
I want to do

Worksheet Twenty-seven: What have you most enjoyed doing?

In this worksheet, write down one or more things you have *most* enjoyed doing in each of three areas of your life (activism, career, and personal). Describe why they satisfied you.

Focus on things you *do*, not merely things you own or things that happen to you, even if the things are a direct or indirect result of your efforts. That is, don't say you enjoyed getting a promotion or a bonus; say you enjoyed the creative process by which you invented a new work system. Don't say you enjoyed winning the election; say what you enjoyed most about your part in the campaign. Don't say you enjoy having a home of your own; say you enjoyed the process of planning it and building it.

Write down as many things as apply — but try to stick with those that give you extraordinary pleasure or satisfaction.

27. In your activism, what have you most enjoyed doing? And why?
In your vocation, what have you most enjoyed doing? And why?
In your personal life, what have you most enjoyed doing? And why?

List any elements that these activities have in common — even connections that seem slight or far-fetched. (For example, that they all involved teamwork, or all were done alone; that they all involved machinery or use of language, etc.) List as many similarities as you can think of.

Worksheet Twenty-eight: What have you most disliked doing?

In this worksheet, write down the things you have most disliked doing in each of three areas of your life (activism, career, and personal). Elaborate upon the reasons you disliked them.

Focus on things you *do*, not merely things that happen to you, even if the thing happens as a direct or indirect result of your efforts. That is, don't say you hated getting chewed out by your boss; say you hated standing on your feet over a hot grill, flipping burgers. Don't say you hated it when your girlfriend left you; say you hated having to fetch and carry for her. Don't say you hated getting arrested in the demonstration, but that you hated participating in violence when your intention was pacifistic.

Write as many things as apply. Again, try to stick to things you really dislike and would prefer to avoid, not just small annoyances.

28. In your activism, what have you most disliked doing? And why?
In your vocation, what have you most disliked doing? And why?
In your personal life, what have you most disliked doing? And why?

List any elements that these activities have in common — even connections that seem slight or far-fetched. (For example, that they all involved bossy people; that they were all boring or too unpredictable; that they caused you to be a hypocrite; that you didn't like how you felt about yourself for having done them, etc.) List as many similarities as you can think of.

Worksheet Twenty-nine: Bringing enjoyable activities to the fore

Now list 10 ways in which you can imagine bringing more of the enjoyable activities of Worksheet Twenty-seven into your life.

As you did with Worksheet Twelve in Chapter Four, try to stay within the bounds of reality — even if you occasionally venture near reality's far borders. For example, to write, "Become independently wealthy" is just an exercise in flippancy unless you have a maiden aunt who's about to die off and leave you all her Microsoft stock, but to say, "Start my own political party" or "Earn 25 percent more than I'm getting now" may be realistic. Even if, in the end, you don't succeed, these are things you can move toward and plan for. Keep in mind your own character and inclinations; write what *you* might want and be able to do.

Also, as you've done before, go ahead and note things you might do, actions you might take, conditions you might change — *even if your pessimistic, burnt out side tells you the effort is "too hard" or "wouldn't work anyway."* Just as long as they are things you can picture your real self doing in the real world.

29. List 10 ways you might be able to bring more of the enjoyable activities of Worksheet Twenty-seven into your life:
1.
2.
3.
4.
5.
6.
7.
8.
9.
10.

Worksheet Thirty: Lessening distasteful activities

Now list 10 ways in which you can imagine eliminating or lessening the impact of the distasteful activities you listed in Worksheet Twenty-eight.

As you did in the previous worksheet, try to stay within the bounds of reality — even if you occasionally venture to reality's far borders. Again, write down things you might really do (or try), even if you're not sure they'd work, even if you're not sure you'll have the energy or the means to achieve them.

30. List 10 ways you might be able to avoid or lessen the distasteful activities of Worksheet Twenty-eight:
1.
2.
3.
4.
5.
6.
7.
8.
9.
10.

Worksheet Thirty-one: Reality time — what I want to do

Review everything you've written in the worksheets above. Also review:

- Worksheet Two, Chapter Two

- Worksheet Eight, Chapter Three

- Worksheets Eleven and Twelve, Chapter Four

- Any notes you've made that pertain to things you might want to do or have

Mining all the information you've written about your likes and dislikes and possible solutions, and any new thoughts that come to mind, compose mini-scenarios of the life you'd like to lead. The following table contains room for one scenario each for your personal life, your work life and your activism. Keep them *active* — that is, once again, focus on what you might *do*, more than things you simply wish would happen to you.

Here are some examples of what a scenario looks like. I'm keeping these short and quite down-to-earth; you may want to go into a lot more detail or to explore more exotic (but please, at least remotely realistic!) territory:

1. Scenario for a satisfying personal life: I would like to move to a small town, but not too far from a major city where I could get an occasional "culture fix." I'd like my wife and me to get counseling to help work out our money problems and to get more help with Michael's schooling. I want to plant a small orchard.

2. Scenario for a satisfying work life: I want to get out of my corporate cubicle, but since I have no desire to go into business for myself, I will look into sales or some other form of field work for my company. I want to cut back my total hours, in the long run, though I'm willing to work more in the short run to make the transition.

3. Scenario for satisfying activism: I will resign as volunteer coordinator for the Phoenix Society because I'm not good at the job and it's a burden, but I'll continue to be a volunteer. Specifically, I'll volunteer to design and print brochures on my computer and to advise the new volunteer coordinator. I'll limit my involvement to 15 hours a month — and I will practice saying NO when asked to do more.

You may want to copy the table and create several sets of scenarios. This could be useful if you want to explore the "feel" of very realistic scenarios vs. more idealistic ones, or if you are so up in the air you need to "try on" several very different plans.

31. Create three scenarios of a more desirable way of life. Write as much detail as you wish. Try to stay within the bounds of what's feasible, even if you don't believe it's immediately attainable.

A more satisfying personal life would be:

A more satisfying work life would be:

A more satisfying form of activism would be:

NOTES: Use this page to make note of anything that struck you while working in this chapter. In particular:

- Any insights into your heart, mind or present circumstances
- Any feelings that came up (particularly any uncomfortable ones)
- Any ideas for things you might like to have, do or be in your future

Chapter Eight
Money, Family and
Other Immovable Objects

It is so easy to get stuck in miserable circumstances. Feeling depressed, at a loss, raging with dissatisfaction — but not knowing what to do.

Some people are stuck for reasons beyond their control — because they're in prison, maybe, or have a disability that keeps them from doing certain things.

Some people are stuck (temporarily) because they've pursued a course of action into a blind alley, or because their priorities are shifting, but their mental compass hasn't yet pointed toward a new path. This probably describes the state of a lot of people reading this book.

Some are stuck (temporarily) because their circumstances have changed and they need time to conceive, then execute, the next move in life.

However, I'm amazed — and honestly, appalled — at the number of people who are stuck just because it's easier to be stuck than to change. "What, me take control of my life? You just don't understand ..."

These "I can't-ers" and "you don't understand-ers" nearly always cite one of three immovable objects by which they believe their lives are permanently fixed:

- Money (lack of)

- Job (silver chains and security blankets)

- Family (ties that bind)

Having cited one or all of the above as their reason for doing nothing, they rapidly revert to whining about how unhappy they are, how they hate their job, how their neighbors are obnoxious, how their kids are demanding little jerks, how miserable their marriage is, what a bunch of backstabbers their co-workers are, or how horrible the state of the world is and-why-doesn't-somebody-(else)-do-something-to-fix-things.

In short, they put enough energy into their "I can'ts" to fuel a good portion of the fulfilling change they believe impossible.

Because you're reading this book, I assume you're not nailed in place with "I can'ts." You want to change your life in positive ways; probably you hope your friends or family will come along with you (or at least cheer you on). The kind and degree of change you need to make, only you can know. If you're fortunate, you just need a change in your political activities to re-vivify your energies, but true burnout may call for major life change — moving to that yurt where you can talk to the birds, giving up the insurance biz for a career as an itinerant artist, getting a divorce, going into (or coming out of) the underground economy.

Like so many other reasons to take the safe, unchanging course, the above three Immovable Objections have a level of undeniable truth — for all of us.

- Unless we're Bill Gates, Ted Turner or a trust-fund baby, lack of money holds us all back.

- Unless we're altogether without personal relationships, family obligations affect everyone to some degree.

- And (see standard exception for Gates, Turner, et al.) we've all got to work to survive.

Every one of us will, in some way, find at least one of the Three Immovable Objects a stumbling block.

Isn't it funny how some people — broke, with family, and needing to earn their daily bread like anyone else — manage to create exciting change, while others in similar circumstances just sit and whine?

Like so many other "truths" we've looked at in this book, the Three Immovable Objects can also function as an excuse, more than as a verity of life.

The bottom line is that all three of those Immovable Objects — and all their cousins — "I don't know how," "but I've lived here all my life," "I'm not trained to do anything else," "I don't have time," "I've always done it this way" — become eminently movable the moment one has the vision and the will to try. Maybe you can only move them a little, teeny way, or maybe you can go crashing through and burst them into a million pieces. That depends.

But move them? Yes, anyone can.

These subjects are too big, too complex, to deal with in this book. So this chapter is here to briefly describe the problem and give you leads to other resources that can help you roll those obstacles out of the way, climb over them, chip them down — or perhaps learn to live with and learn to admire them, if that's what you ultimately choose to do.

The Money Obstacle

The money objection has a lot of forms: "Too much debt." "I don't make enough." "Money's all tied up in investments." "My parents won't give me any." "I'm secure now; why should I take a risk?" "It costs too much to do what I really want to do."

Ad infinitum and *ad nauseum*.

Let's keep in mind that almost nobody has the money they really need to fulfill their dreams, and that your work in this book is intended to produce "gymnastics training" kind of changes, not magic bullet kinds of changes. That said, what can you do when a lack of money holds you back?

- First, analyze how much of your dilemma is truly lack of money and how much is your attitude — which may be keeping you from taking even initial steps toward change. Even if you're really poor, you can start envisioning a new path and beginning planning for it. This is hard — but worth doing.

- Second, figure out where your specific money problems lie (job that pays less than your capabilities merit, too many credit cards, too much "fun" spending, drinking and partying, rent on an upscale apartment, legal bills, spending for psychological comfort or status, taxes too high, etc.).

- Third, start tackling the part of the problem that's easiest to handle. If you're really bad off, that might simply mean making sure that that problem doesn't get *worse* for the time being. (Been there; done that, too.) Even that, however, is progress.

- Help for these steps and much more can be found in the book *Your Money or Your Life* by Vicki Robin and the late Joe Dominguez. I've recommended this book to the point where regular readers might be sick of hearing about it, but there's nothing like it for 1) giving you a systematic and sensible way of evaluating your finances; 2) changing your entire life's relationship to money; and 3) making it joyfully clear that your life will be improved in every way when you're done.

I bow to Robin and Dominguez when it comes to a great system for moving The Money Obstacle. The main thing is to recognize that, in a vast and varied world, and with people as willing to go out on the edge as we, there are *always* ways out. Your particular solutions will be governed by your psychology and your circumstances. No matter how dire things look, you can move this obstacle.

The only sin against yourself is to sit there and do nothing.

The Job Obstacle

"Risk these great benefits? No way." "I've got student loans to pay." "I'm doing this because my parents always wanted me to be a [fill in the blank]." "It's a drag, but another job might be worse." "My boss would never allow me to telecommute." "You've just got to face reality." "Well, it ain't much, but it makes the payments on my Porsche." "I have to provide for my children." "I'm not trained to do anything else."

The Job Obstacle, too, takes dozens of forms, and has thousands of potential solutions. In making major life change, you might need to:

- Quit your job altogether
- Reduce your hours to have time for other things
- Ease into a less stressful position
- Go into business for yourself
- Get a new job with an activist group or non-profit organization
- Boost your hours or your wages to help move The Money Obstacle
- Retrain for something more satisfying.

Above all, if you're in a job that's grinding you down, you're depleting at least half your waking life — and contributing hugely to the burnout we've been pondering.

Only you can decide whether you want to go on trading that much of your existence for whatever benefits you're getting from your employment. Perhaps you do, and will continue to want to. Perhaps you have a great job. Perhaps it isn't great, but it pays so well you'd be nuts to leave (yet). Perhaps it's building your reputation. Many people see their jobs as the fixed point around which the rest of their lives revolve. Quitting that job would be the *last* thing you'd want to do if you're about to make choices that might involve risk. God knows you don't have to leave a job to be fulfilled.

However, if your job is contributing to your burnout and you believe it is necessary to find something better or to make some adjustment, like a job share, flex time or telecommuting (*even* if you can't begin to conceive how to move this particular large purple elephant in your path), start thinking, talk to your boss, talk to your partner, and — when you need full-immersion therapy for a major job shift:

Hit the library.

The tiny town library where I roam has *nine full shelves* devoted to work — job hunting, job interviews, job skills, job types, starting businesses, working from home, working in technology, leading, managing, communicating, working in arts & crafts, etc. That's not counting all the hundreds of books in that same itty-bitty library on how to *run* your own business once you've chosen to start one.

If you know or believe you're going to need to take the ultimate step — leaving a secure job — the best career-changing book is still Richard Nelson Bolles' always-updated gem, *What Color Is Your Parachute?* These days it's really two books bound into one (the main book and a workbook and resource guide of equal length). *Parachute* is particularly good for anyone who's majorly up in the air about questions like "What do I really enjoy doing?" and "Where in the world do I want to work?" *Parachute*, with its mix of professional savvy, practical advice and flights of visionary thinking, is like nothing else. Read it first, then hit those nine shelves again when you start to narrow down your career search.

The Family Obstacle

"My wife won't go along with me." "I don't want to disrupt my children's lives." "My parents are old and need me." "My asshole parents say I can't." "I'm too busy driving the kids to soccer practice." "My husband is a control freak." "Maybe after I've gotten the kids through Harvard." "Guilt trips!"

Of the Three Immovable Objects, The Family Obstacle is, without a doubt, the hardest to move, especially if you have children, elderly parents who need your care, or if you come from a family that devoted several decades to manipulating you into living your entire life as An Obligation. When you want to make changes in your life, you affect all these people like the proverbial falling dominoes

When one person makes sweeping changes in attitude or behavior, it has the potential to blow the whole family apart — or at least throw it into serious unbalance. Some classic examples are:

- When one member of a couple who've lived a freewheeling life "gets religion." (Or gives up recreational chemicals.) Suddenly, the two not only have little in common, but the "reformed" member often drives her former partner-in-play crazy with proselytizing.

- When a man seeking personal fulfillment quits his job to do something less lucrative, leaving spouse and kids in narrow straits that were not of their own choosing.

- When Dad or Mom walks away in the name of fulfillment.

The kind of changes you may be contemplating may also have such real, and grave impacts. As often as not, however, the threats to dependents are more psychological than actual. For example:

- Your interests diverge, leaving your partner feeling he doesn't know you anymore;

- A partner perceives that your changing goals may threaten her security, status or relationships with other family members (even if they haven't actually);

- A partner feels fearful and out of control because he doesn't share the changes you're so enthused about. Or doesn't even understand them and just wants you to go back to being the way you were.

- Children receive the emotional backlash of any of the above.

Unlike The Money Obstacle, you can't just systematically determine to gain control of The Family Obstacle and start moving. Unlike the Job Obstacle, you can't just …well, say, "shove it." Family is a complex structure of dependencies, demands, obligations, emotions, and mutual support, and within it can't just seek your own Total Fulfillment to the neglect of your dependents or partners — unless you're a real jerk, or unless your family members are ready for your independence.

If you must weave a path of self-fulfillment around the needs of children or aging parents, you may have to settle for the most imperfect and fragmentary personal change. (Hopefully, you accepted that when you chose the obligation.) On the other hand, fulfilling your obligations to them may be the greatest self-fulfillment in the world.

In any case, one excellent way to start pushing at this particular Immovable Object is by dividing your family obligations into two broad areas: 1) People who are genuinely dependent on you — that is, who for reasons *beyond their control* would have great difficulty surviving without your presence and support — and, 2) people who are in your life but who have their own interests, needs *and* capacity for taking care of themselves (or being well taken care of by others). The first group, you may have to plan around,[1] but the second group you might be able to talk with,[2] reason with, or find entirely new paths with.

You may even end up forging a mutual understanding and agreement that will enrich your journey.

On the other hand, you may end up splitting, or coming up with some workable compromise. At the very least you will have brought your concerns and desires out in the open where they can be dealt with.

Even if your relationship with your dependents turns out to be an Immovable Obstacle that you can only just barely manage to nudge a few inches, you're that far ahead, after all.

When it comes to finding self-fulfillment while dealing with a partner, friends or grown children, there's no one great guide, as there is for dealing with money or jobs. However, here are a few good books that might help:

Choice Theory: A New Psychology of Personal Freedom by William Glasser (about letting go of attempts to control others), *Straight from the Heart* by Layne and Paul Cutright (which emphasizes clear communication between partners and offers simple tools to help), *Too Good to Leave, Too Bad to Stay* by Mira Kirshenbaum (a self-help guide to deciding whether or not a relationship is salvageable), *Simple Loving: A Path to Deeper, More Sustainable Relationships* by Janet Luhrs (which comes out of the same voluntary simplicity movement that produced *Your Money* and may not be for everybody), *If the Buddha Dated: A Handbook for Finding Love on a Spiritual Path* by Charlotte Kasl, Ph.D. (a light-hearted, simple, but ultimately serious guide not only to dating, but to enriching all kinds of relationships). And though it's become almost cliché to recommend it, John Gray's *Men Are From Mars, Women Are From Venus*. If you're in a heterosexual relationship, nothing is better for helping you communicate with a mate.

If your personal journey carries you away from your partner[3] try reading *Rebuilding: When Your Relationship Ends* by Bruce Fisher and Robert E. Alberti. It's one of the most helpful resources for handling divorce or separation.

---

[1] Unless you discover that the dependency is unwarranted — say an adult child who won't let go (but needs to), a drug-addicted sibling who holds you through a lifelong habit of obligation, or a healthy, middle-aged parent who holds you only through guile and guilt. You would do very well to shake off such "imposed dependencies" — and the addicted, unmotivated, manipulative people on the receiving end of your decision might benefit, as well.

[2] Yes, though those of us raised in dysfunctional families find it hard to imagine, in some families, the members actually do talk. (As opposed to screaming, blaming and inventing scurrilous epithets for one another.) As an adult, my Significant Sweetie and I discovered to our surprise that actual talk seems to be the finest way to *prevent* dysfunctional familyism and set mutual goals.

[3] Or if your partner puts up with the new you for about two minutes before pitching your socks and your CD player out in the driveway.

One thing affects another

One thing you may have noticed is how closely related the money-family-job obstacles are: You need the job because it takes so much money to keep your children in Nikes. The job pays well, but you only keep it because your wife thinks it's important. Your father-in-law gave you the job because you were otherwise so hopeless at earning money.

You could think of that as complicated. It certainly makes it harder when you begin to think how you'll approach your first Immovable. ("I know; I'll quit Microsoft and buy that leather-working shop in Montana ...but the kids would be torn out of school ...and we need my husband's salary ...and.")

You might also think of it as holistic. Quite possibly, as you move one of the Immovable Objects, the others may surprise you by sliding out of your way on their own — at least far enough to let you see a ray of light on the other side. Particularly if you can get your family with you, the other obstacles may seem less formidable.

A break! No worksheets in this chapter.

In this chapter, we're barely touching on three complex, highly charged topics. And they are topics that have vastly different ramifications for every reader. No handful of worksheets could begin to fill your needs if you are contemplating major assaults on any of the Immovable Objects. That would take a book, and another book, and another book.

Fortunately, at least two of the books mentioned above have extensive worksheets to get you where you need to go.

For moving Money Obstacles, Robin and Dominguez' *Your Money or Your Life* contains very useful and detailed planners to help you track your spending habits, then analyze how your spending fits into your life values.

The Parachute Workbook (bound with *What Color Is Your Parachute?*) contains a wonderful — though misleadingly named — "Quick Job-Hunting Map." The map is not quick at all; the needed self-analysis could take you days (but those days would be well spent). Nor does it apply only to job hunters; it could be adaptable to anyone contemplating major life changes. By covering everything from your entire life's skill-building to your concept of spirituality and the meaning of life, then wrapping it all up in one diagram, it gives you a fine aid to determining what you really want to do — and why.

The worksheets in Chapter Six of *Think Free to Live Free* — though set up to help you analyze your political activities — might also be of use to prospective career changers.

If anyone finds a true workbook to creating healthy personal change within the context of relationships — particularly one that is as real-world useful as *Parachute* or *Your Money*, let my publisher know.

In the meantime, some of the worksheets in Chapter Nine will help you plan ways to get past many types of obstacles — including these.

Chapter Nine
Planning for Action

Now it's time to put it all together — to set a goal and make an action plan for getting there.

It's still perfectly okay at this point if you aren't ready to set a "real" goal. Going from Chapter One to Chapter Nine in a book does not mean going from burnout hell to fireball energy. It doesn't mean you've gone from cross-eyed confusion to having a clear view of the future. If that's happened, great! I'm glad for you, and glad this book worked so well. However, it's just as likely that you'll still need more time to reflect on these worksheets and to ruminate about the thoughts and ideas they aroused in you before you can say, "This is what I want."

If you're unready now, you may wake up at midnight three months from now with some insight based on the thoughts you had while working through Chapter Three or Four or Seven and suddenly see your situation in a different light. *Then* you'll be ready to make a real action plan.[1] But ...

Whether you feel ready for action at the moment or not,

DON'T skip the worksheets in this chapter.

DON'T put them off, saying, "I'll do them when I'm more prepared" or "I'll do them when I'm feeling less depressed." Or whatever.

If you're still frazzled or up in the air at the moment, fine. Relax and let it be. But use the following worksheets as an *exercise in practical thinking*. Pick a goal that feels possible and right for you, even if it isn't "the" ultimate goal, and go through the process contained in this chapter.

By working through these exercises — goal setting, recognizing limitations and obstacles, planning practical steps — you're setting some productive mental patterns — even if you aren't ready to take the actual steps.

If you are ready — go for it!

There's not much else to say now. If you've come this far, you're ready to begin creating the vision of a future and planning steps that can take you there.

---

[1] Or perhaps you'll find that your unconscious mind has been working on one all along, without notifying your waking self about it until that moment.

Not the linear type?

This chapter asks you to do some linear thinking: How do I get from here to there via steps A, B, and C?

Some people are very comfortable with that kind of thinking. But — harking back to Chapter Two and our talk of temperaments — others are more intuitive and may object that linear planning kills creativity or eliminates the possibility of joyful serendipity.

I know the objection is out there because I'm one of those intuitive (and impulsive) sorts myself. Nevertheless, I'm all for linear planning even if, for people like us, the plan is less something we follow than something we weave around.

Thinking out a course of future activity does not kill creativity — because it is, in itself, a creative act. (Any writer or artist will tell you that our much vaunted "inspiration" rarely comes when we're staring at clouds or picking daisies; it comes when we're sitting at the computer or in the studio kicking around ideas or fiddling with colors and textures, or it strikes us while we're in the daisy field, but only *because* of work we've been doing in the studio or at the computer. That's what you're doing here; fiddling with possibilities.)

And planning doesn't eliminate serendipity because you can always deviate from a planned course when a better option presents itself.

I know us creative/intuitive types. Without something anchoring us (in this case, anchoring us to a future vision) we're likely to drift aimlessly — following "inspiration" and "serendipity" right into nowhere and nothingness. I've also known too many people — intuitive types or otherwise — who use their desire for "spontaneity" as an excuse to do nothing useful. *Planning? How dull. How routine. I think I'll just sit here and wait for the cosmos to send me a message ...*

So, you fellow creative types and you lazy excuse makers: Get linear! (For the moment, anyway.)

Worksheet Thirty-two: Setting a long-term goal

Look back to Worksheet Thirty-one in Chapter Seven, where you wrote down a set (or several sets) of scenarios for your life, your work and your activism.

Now, mine those scenarios to create a goal for what you'd like to have/do/be when you emerge from your burnout. This goal may encompass elements from any of your mini-scenarios and may apply to any (or all) parts of your life. You should keep it fairly simple. Make it something you can realistically work toward (even if you don't have confidence you can actually achieve it).

The statement you write here is going to function as your working goal for the rest of this chapter, so you shouldn't daunt yourself with detail. It should have one central point, or at most two or three aspects, like the following samples:

- My goal is to live quietly with my family and to eliminate as many as possible of the demands that take me away from them.

- My goal is to be single again, move to Washington D.C., and to get a job that lets me be paid for working on the political issues that matter to me.

- My goal is to put everything aside for a while and spend a year hitchhiking around the world.

- My goal is to have time to create hand-made furniture.

- My goal is to return to medical school.

- My goal is to persuade my girlfriend to return to me, while at the same time finding some way to pursue my career and my convictions without neglecting our relationship.

- My goal is to be elected to the state assembly.

In setting this goal, also keep in mind your basic temperament characteristics from Chapter Two, your value statements from Chapter Three and any of the "crazy-makers" you listed in Chapter Four. The reason to give your goals a Reality Check against your temperament and values is that we sometimes think we want to achieve, or have, things we really wouldn't like if we got them. A minor example: You imagine you'd like more quiet time to meditate, but every time you sit still for five minutes, your active nature leaves you restless and bored. Do you really want meditation time (as sort of a personal discipline)? Are you just thinking wishfully? The reason to give your goals a Reality Check against your "crazy-makers" is to examine whether the goal you state might lead you right back into the circumstances you hate. (Not likely; but it could happen.)

How real is this goal?

It's great if the goal you work with here is your real one (or *a* real one). It should certainly be something that is likely to be what you really want to achieve.

But remember, even if you feel unready to fix on a long-term goal, it is important to do this as an exercise — like trying on a pair of shoes to see how they fit you.

Do not neglect or postpone this step or any of the worksheets in this chapter. If "thinking free" is to lead to "acting free," you must internalize the desire to *act*, not merely to sit and *think*. This chapter is critical to doing that.

32. My goal is ...

Worksheet Thirty-three: Overcoming limitations and obstructions

Before you go on to working out the steps needed to get where you want to go, stop and take a look at the barriers you perceive to progress.

Before you do this, you may want to review:

- Worksheet Three, Chapter Two
- Worksheets Six, Seven and Eight, Chapter Three
- All the worksheets in Chapter Four
- Worksheets Thirteen and Fourteen in Chapter Five
- Any of the worksheets in Chapter Seven

You've already done part of the task of defining your personal obstacles in those sections.

Your mission here (should you choose to accept it) is to state the most *serious* limitations and obstructions standing between you and your goal, then to propose at least one action — and preferably three — you could take to overcome it.

Limitations, barriers or obstructions might take many forms. They could be psychological, financial, physical, religious, practical or of any other nature. They could be related to temperament, relationships, morality, handicaps, personal weaknesses, bad people — anything you perceive to be strongly holding you back or standing in your way.

Examples of these obstacles include (but are far from limited to — it all depends on your goal and your circumstances): My beliefs don't permit X; I can't sell my house quickly; I have dependent children; I can't break my commitment to the party; I don't have the money; I'm not aggressive by nature; I don't have the stamina; it requires a medical degree; the police are watching me; I haven't established my credibility; I'm allergic to X; the telephone company is beaming microwaves into my brain (just kidding); there's a large amount of luck required; my boss's wife is a harpy; I'm afraid of catching a tropical disease; I live in the wrong country — and of course, the ever-popular "no money!"

Ways of overcoming obstacles are also nearly unlimited (although, alas, they sometimes seem all too limited) and will depend on your circumstances and ingenuity. The most important thing to understand is that "overcoming" doesn't necessarily mean conquering the thing standing in your way. It could mean going *around* an obstacle. Perhaps coming up with a partial solution to a problem. It could mean making changes in your lifestyle or simply waiting until a problem goes away. It could mean committing some clever act of deception, like changing your identity. It could mean an act of non-violent sabotage, a culture-jamming prank that brings down an enemy. It could mean making a temporary alliance to get past a barrier, or somehow turning a barrier to your advantage (as a ju-jitsu practitioner turns his opponent's strength against him).

In this table, write any serious obstacles you can think of in the left-hand column. Then note any solutions you can think of on the right. Again, feel free to propose solutions you don't really have confidence in — as long as they are something you (not Superman) could conceivably do.

Your solutions don't have to be entirely practical.

You don't have to "believe" in them at this point.

But they should be doable by someone like you.

If, when you've finished the exercise, you haven't been able to think of *any* solutions to one or more of your most pressing obstacles, then you either need to go back to Worksheet Thirty-two and choose a goal that's more within the realm of reality, or you need to think more creatively.

There is no point whatsoever to defining a goal that is beyond all possibility of attainment.

Yes, perhaps it's true that your reach should exceed your grasp. After all, we humans are prone to get bored and inert if we achieve what we want too easily. That's not usually the activist's problem. Since *our* problem tends to be wanting the moon, then failing either to get it or to go for it at all, we need to learn a more down-to-earth kind of goal setting.

Hint: You can stimulate creative thinking by grabbing a sheet of notebook paper, taking a deep breath, relaxing and just writing down any "solutions" (however far out) that may come to mind. Write rapidly and don't think too hard. By the time you've written several dozen — or a hundred — wild and random "solutions" (which usually doesn't take much time at all once you're "in the flow"), you'll probably have come up with one or two practical ones. At worst, you'll have come up with a couple of wild ones that at least *point the way* toward an answer your linear mind wouldn't have come up with.

I've given you seven blanks for obstacles. Note as few or as many obstacles as apply in your case. Use extra paper if you need to.

Here goes ...

33. The biggest obstacles between me and my goal are:	I might solve them by:
1.	1. 2. 3.
2.	1. 2. 3.
3.	1. 2. 2.
4.	1. 2. 3.
5.	1. 2. 3.
6.	1. 2. 3.
7.	1. 2. 3.

When you are satisfied that you have at least some potential "obstacle buster" for every major obstacle standing between you and your goal, it's time to move on to the next stage.

Worksheet Thirty-four: Choosing interim goals

Now, based on your goal statement from Worksheet Thirty-two, select several *interim* goals that fall between your present circumstances and your long-term goal. I've given space for five, but you may have as few as one or as many as you need. Write the goal on the left and the approximate time to reach it on the right.

At this point, don't write down the *actions* you'll take to reach those interims. Interim goals are the *stages you could reach,* not the actions. (Note: The stages are more important than the time frames. You should never let yourself become fatally discouraged merely because something doesn't happen as quickly as you want it to; the important thing is where you're headed, not when you get there.)

Note: You *may* want to do this worksheet *after* you do Worksheet Thirty-five. A lot will depend on your personal planning style.

Here's an example of a set of interim goals, based on the person who wants to eliminate demands on her life and spend more time with family:

Sample only	
Right now, I am too busy, too tired, too wrapped up in office politics, too overcommitted with political/volunteer work, too alienated from my kids.	**Estimated time to reach**
Interim goal #1 Finish and be free of all volunteer obligations.	Six months
Interim goal #2 Have car paid off.	Nine months
Interim goal #3 Be in a position to cut back my hours at work to no more than 40; have someone trained to carry the excess.	One year & two months
Interim goal #4 Have friends and distant relatives conditioned to know I won't be as available to them.	Gradual process! Constant!
Interim goal #5 Achieve job share; work no more than 25 hours a week. Return to some activist work on a limited, carefully chosen basis.	One year, six months
The Goal Time, time, time! Time for my family.	One year, six months

Your turn ...

34. Right now, I am	Estimated time to reach
Interim goal #1	
Interim goal #2	
Interim goal #3	
Interim goal #4	
Interim goal #5	
The Goal	

Worksheet Thirty-five: Getting into action

To reach each interim goal you'll have a set of actions to perform.

As I planned these worksheets, I found myself having a surprising amount of trouble deciding whether this worksheet should come before or after the worksheet on interim goal setting.

Super-linear organizers among this book's readers may say that *naturally* interim goals come first — that you can't even decide which steps to take until you know where you're going. Such enviable folks will plan every step *now* and carry on like Patton grinding his way across Sicily.

For most of us, the process is more complex: Deciding what steps to take tells us where we're likely to reach interim goals, and reaching (or even thinking about) interim goals will help us decide what steps to take. It can go both ways and all ways at once.

For instance, I may not have the slightest idea what my first interim goal should be, but I may overwhelmingly understand that my first *action* must be to tell that demanding co-worker to go take a …er, a long, well-deserved vacation, and that my second step is to analyze how I got involved in such a crummy organization in the first place. Only after I've taken those steps may I have the clarity to know that my interim goal is: "Get out of Organization X."

On the other hand, if I already know (or strongly feel) that my first goal should be to "Get out of Organization X," then only after that do I decide which steps to take to make a graceful exit.

So you see, it's a very personal thing, whether you set goals first or decide steps first. You may be constantly re-evaluating interim goals and necessary steps as you work toward your main goal.

The main thing to remember is:

Action steps lead to interim goals.

Interim goals signal time to take new action steps.

So in this exercise, we'll first list a number of steps to take along the path to our goal — without regard to whether Step A leads to Interim Goal C, or Step G leads to Interim Goal A.

Then, and only then, will we integrate steps and goals — keeping in mind that such integration is tentative at this stage and always subject to thoughtful re-evaluation and/or the workings of serendipity.

Note: The best of your "obstacle busters" from Worksheet Thirty-three will probably show up again here — along with some easier actions you can take on the way to your goal. In coming up with action ideas, you can also consult:

- Worksheet Eight, Chapter Three
- Worksheet Twelve, Chapter Four
- Worksheets Twenty-four and Twenty-five, Chapter Six
- All worksheets in Chapter Seven
- Any notes you've made pertaining to things you might want to do.

35. To travel from my present state to my long-term goal, here are ten actions I could perform:

1.

2.

3.

4.

5.

6.

7.

8.

9.

10.

Worksheet Thirty-six: Integrating interim goals and action steps

Now, look at your interim goals from Worksheet Thirty-four, then look at the actions you wrote down in Worksheet Thirty-five. List the goals in their order, and insert the steps where you believe they belong.

You'll almost certainly observe that your 10 steps from Worksheet Thirty-five don't constitute a complete action plan. It's likely that some of your steps won't fit at all, and extremely likely that you'll have a lot of beginning steps or easy steps and still feel completely clueless about other steps.

In the following table, insert additional steps where you discover a need for them. Don't worry if steps are missing at this point (unless they're major, deal-killer type steps like "Get a million dollars" or "Become incredibly charismatic" or "Stop sinning" — you probably aren't helping yourself by including those kinds of steps, anyway).

You don't need to know every step before you begin moving. New steps — and new opportunities — will reveal themselves as you move along your path. Unexpected job offers, new relationships, healing techniques, helping hands, surprise political developments may all shape your eventual actions.

What you are doing here is an exercise. But *do* use it as a guide to making your early steps. And *do* return to it for periodic re-evaluations and changes. Certainly return to it each time you meet (or are about to meet) one of your interim goals, so that you can determine whether the upcoming goals and actions are still appropriate.

36. Right now, I am	Estimated time to reach
Steps to Interim goal #1	
Interim goal #1	
Steps to Interim goal #2	
Interim goal #2	
Steps to Interim goal #3	
Interim goal #3	
Steps to Interim goal #4	
Interim goal #4	
Steps to Interim goal #5	
Interim goal #5	
Steps to The Goal	
The Goal	

Worksheet Thirty-seven: What my goal means to me

Now, you have a path to take. Perhaps at this stage you're still tired, lacking confidence and feeling daunted by the task ahead. Nobody ever claimed that setting a reasonable goal and taking steps toward it was easy — or that a handful of worksheets could solve every dilemma.

What I will say is that, if you want to live free — to live with as much integrity, happiness, effectiveness, and clarity as your nature allows — you need first to Know Thyself, then to *act* on what you know, what you are best at, what you desire and what you value. Easy? Hell no! Inertia is far more comfortable. Remaining miserable is a nice, safe course — which many choose. Doing nothing involves less risk. Blaming others for your failure to live your convictions or your desires is downright luxurious.

Still, thinking with clarity, then acting on what you know — even if it takes extraordinary courage — is the most worthwhile course. It's a course life and human nature will constantly try to pull you away from.

So one last exercise — and perhaps you should tape this worksheet to your bathroom mirror when you've completed it.

Write down why it's important to you to reach your goal. Pour out all your present (and past) frustration, fear, anguish, and exhaustion. Pour out your hopes and dreams. Let the future shine over your past and present. Envision what you want to achieve. Understand and remember the glowing value of it.

Let it be your guiding star:

37. I aim for my goal because ...

NOTES: Use this page to make note of anything that struck you while working in this chapter. In particular:

- Any insights into your heart, mind or present circumstances

- Any feelings that came up (particularly any uncomfortable ones)

- Any ideas for things you might like to have, do or be in your future

Resources

Finding out more about yourself

Websites:

http://www.keirsey.com/cgi-bin/newkts.cgi — Keirsey Temperament Sorter. A free web-based temperament inventory. Dr. Keirsey calls it an improvement on the original Myers-Briggs typology, and it uses the famous Myers-Briggs types.

http://www.personalitytype.com — Five-minute mini-test for determining your Myers-Briggs personality (temperament) type.

http://www.queendom.com — General personality, interest, IQ and other tests at Cyberia Shrink's Queendom.

http://www.trans4mind.com/personality/ A quite different type of free personality inventory.

Books:

Introduction to Type: A guide to understanding your results on the Myers-Briggs type indicator, by Isabel Briggs Myers.

Please Understand Me: Character and temperament types, by David Keirsey and Marilyn Bates.

The Outsider, by Colin Wilson. The classic study from the 1950s of the person who stands alone in literature and in life.

Changing your life

Note: While there are plenty of legitimate self-transformation programs that require you to pay a fee, please beware of the phonies or vapor-vendors. Any time you sense that a program peddler is more interested in 1) money; and 2) airy, New-Agey promises than in solid information and value-for-value, run like hell.

Websites and online courses:

http://www.selfgrowth.com/ — Selfgrowth.com. An Internet portal to all things related to self-transformation, be it exercise and health, addiction and recovery, speed-reading, general self-improvement or spirituality.

http://www.trans4mind.com/ — Tools for Transformation. A wide-ranging site that features downloadable courses (not free!) and information about techniques such as meta-programming and psycho-linguistics.

http://www.cise.ufl.edu/~ddd/12step.html — Harvey Fierstein's 12-Step Program to Change your Life. Brief and amusing, as well as perfectly commonsensical.

Books:

Change Your Life and Everyone in It: How to transform difficult relationships, overcome anxiety and depression, break free from self-defeating ways, by Michele Weiner-Davis. It comes highly recommended as a practical guide to building on what is positive in your life.

Your Money or Your Life, by Vicki Robin and Joe Dominguez. Incredible guide to transforming your relationship with money. This is *not* a book on budgeting (though it will help you do that), but a book on satisfaction, meaning, commitment and regaining control of many aspects of your life.

Getting involved; finding a new volunteer activity or a job

Websites:

http://www.idealist.org — Guide to volunteer organizations of all types in all corners of the world — more than 20,000 of them. Idealist also features listings of paying jobs and consulting opportunities with non-profit groups. This is without question the finest resource listed under this heading.

http://www.jobhuntersbible.com/ — Richard Nelson Bolle's online supplement to his classic and invaluable employment guide, *What Color Is Your Parachute?* Contains plenty of resources on career development, interactive personality & interest tests, links to job listings, etc.

Books:

What Color Is Your Parachute?, by Richard Nelson Bolles. Find a job. Find yourself while on your way to your new vocation.

I was unable to locate a *general* printed guide to activism or volunteerism (though a search of Amazon.com or your local library will reveal a wealth of books on community building, leadership and related topics). If anyone is aware of a book to help activists of all stripes get active and be effective, please let me know through my publisher. In the meantime, if you have access to the Web, Idealist.org's guide to books, videos and articles will go a long way toward making up for the absence of a comprehensive manual.

It's also a telling commentary that nearly every activist book available is geared to one side of the political spectrum. Among those, the following are worth a look:

The Activist's Handbook: A Primer for the 1990s and Beyond, by Randy Shaw. Geared to those interested in environmental causes, poverty, minorities, etc. Contains practical information on getting things done, dealing with the press, etc.

Rules for Radicals, by Saul Alinsky. Dated, but still potent tactical manual for non-mainstream activists.

One classic of idealism that defies categorization is:

Community Technology, by Karl Hess, with an introduction by Carole Moore. A hopelessly idealistic, but inspiring guide to transforming a community through neighborhood-based industry. Hess' thesis was that communities must control their own means of production if they are to avoid being controlled politically (and every other way) from outside.

Other Titles of Interest:

101 THINGS TO DO 'TIL THE REVOLUTION
Ideas and resources for self-liberation, monkey wrenching and preparedness
by Claire Wolfe

We don't need a weatherman to know which way the wind blows — but we do need the likes of Claire Wolfe, whose book offers 101 suggestions to help grease the wheels as we roll towards the government's inevitable collapse. Wolfe's list is lengthy and thought-provoking, as she elaborates on each piece of advice, from generalities to precise instructions. For the concerned citizen who wishes to keep a low profile, protect his or her rights, and survive in the "interesting times" which are sure to come, this is essential reading. *1996, 5½ x 8½, 216 pp, soft cover.* **Order Number 94281. $15.95.**

DON'T SHOOT THE BASTARDS (YET)
101 More Ways to Salvage Freedom
by Claire Wolfe

In this follow-up to Claire Wolfe's widely popular *101 Things To Do 'Til The Revolultion*, she provides more ways to monkeywrench a system that keeps citizens in a stranglehold. She teaches how to prepare for a truly independent lifestyle, and imparts further insight on how to liberate people from the Powers that Be. You can wax on about freedom. You can whine about government rules. But the only way to change the way things are is to take action against the Tyranny traipsing all over American lives. This book is the best place to start. *1999, 5½ x 8½, 249 pp, soft cover.* **Order Number 94304. $15.95.**

COMMUNITY TECHNOLOGY
by Karl Hess
with an Introduction by Carol Moore

In the 1970s, the late Karl Hess participated in a five-year social experiment in Washington D.C.'s Adams-Morgan neighborhood. Hess and several thousand others labored to make their neighborhood as self-sufficient as possible, turning to such innovative techniques as raising fish in basements, growing crops on rooftops and in vacant lots, installing self-contained bacteriological toilets, and planning a methanol plant to convert garbage to fuel. There was a newsletter and weekly community meetings, giving Hess and others a taste of participatory government that changed their lives forever. *1979, 5½ x 8½, 120 pp, soft cover.* **Order Number 14177. $9.95.**

NATIVE AMERICAN ANARCHISM
by Eunice Minette Schuster

Anarchism has exploded into the forefront of today's political movements? What are the roots of those movements? This book discusses the history of anarchism in the United States from colonial times to the early 20th Century. It covers the abolitionists, women's rights movements; supporters of reproductive and sexual freedom; pacifist and anti-war movements; alternative communities and much more. Native American Anarchism is not only an important historical book for contemporary radicals — it's also enjoyable and exciting reading. *1932, 5½ x 8½, 202 pp, soft cover.* **Order Number 94068. $12.00.**

ANARCHIC HARMONY
The Spirituality of Social Disobedience
by William J Murray
Introduction by Robert Anton Wilson

The author writes: "What I found by turning my back on our society-generated mythology was so profound that I had to share it — presumptuous or not — because it *indicts the social structures of mankind* and *demands social disobedience,* or living according to our inner, *heroic nature* and *not* according to the intimidation and demands of society's ideology. Rediscovering your designed purpose by stripping away the false programming of society, abandoning the errant belief systems and embarking upon a path of honest observation and self-discovery is what is meant by social disobedience." *1992, 5½ x 8½, 129 pp, soft cover.* **Order Number 94187. $12.95.**

UNCONDITIONAL FREEDOM
Social Revolution Through Individual Empowerment
by William J Murray
with an Introduction by Ben G. Price

In *Anarchic Harmony*, Murray shattered the myths of the New Age and the old, showing us how to find our Inner Dynamic and use it as our only barometer of right and wrong. Now he teaches us how to manipulate reality to gain unlimited freedom. "We're going to knock down the walls and rip up the floorboards that keep us imprisoned in the hellish box of 'normal life' and consensus reality," says the author. That's something worth reading, don't you think? *1993, 5½ x 8½, 260 pp, soft cover.* **Order Number 94222. $16.95.**

Selections From FREE AMERICA
by Bolton Hall

Bolton Hall was a pioneer in "alternative economics" at the turn of the century. One of the most creative thinkers of his time, he rubbed elbows with the likes of Emma Goldman and Benjamin Tucker. These 20 essays cover subjects such as taxes, cooperative living, political reform, money reform, monopolies, free trade, and much more, including an introduction by Mark Sullivan. "So long as law-created conditions prevent the masses from acquiring intelligence for useful purposes, so long will it be impossible to have clean politics." — Bolton Hall. *5½ x 8½, 199 pp, illustrated, soft cover.* **Order Number 94105. $8.95.**

THE MYTH OF NATURAL RIGHTS
by L.A. Rollins

Once you've read this book, you'll be able to put those imaginary protectors of freedom back in the museums whence they came. In this seminal work, L.A. Rollins effectively demolishes the myth of "natural rights." He exposes the "bleeding heart libertarians" who promote these rights, including Ayn Rand, Murray Rothbard, Tibor Machan, Samuel Konkin and others. Rollins dissects the arguments for natural rights, cutting through the faulty logic to the core of libertarian dogma. An important book for libertarians who take their ideas seriously. *1983, 5½ x 8½, 50 pp, soft cover.* **Order Number 94067. $7.95.**

NATURAL LAW
or Don't Put a Rubber on Your Willy
by Robert Anton Wilson

A continuing episode in the critique of natural rights theories started by L.A. Rollins' *The Myth of Natural Rights,* Wilson lets fly at Murray Rothbard, George Smith, Samuel Konkin and other purveyors of the "claim that some sort of metaphysical entity called a 'right' resides in a human being like a 'ghost' residing in a haunted house." An entertaining, informative and well-thought out book that should be read by anyone who has ever been attracted to *any* ideology. *1987, 5½ x 8½, 72 pp, soft cover.* **Order Number 94101. $7.95.**

RESIST NOT EVIL
by Clarence Darrow
Introduction by Carol Moore

Clarence Darrow is best known for defending the right to teach evolution in "the Scopes trial." Not so well-known is his lifetime of service on behalf of victims of government persecution. In *Resist Not Evil*, Darrow presents a convincing case for abolishing the criminal justice system. Darrow argues that neither punishment nor prison reduce the crime rate, and the only reason for them is vengeance and cruelty. He points out that most crimes are committed against property by people who have been shut out of the economic system. This reprint of Darrow's controversial essay could not be more timely; his ideas have lost none of their fire or relevance. *1902, 5½ x 8½, 188 pages, indexed, soft cover.* **Order Number 99099. $11.95.**

HARD CORE
Marginalized by Choice
by P.J. Nebergall

Hard Core: Marginalized by Choice is a photojournalistic odyssey into the Punk world that permeates our current intercultural milieu. P.J. Nebergall has placed the modern Punk phenomenon in its proper historical perspective by conducting hundreds of interviews and photo shoots with rebellious and disenchanted youngsters in both Great Britain and the United States. His text and photographs provide a penetrating glimpse into the philosophical musings and neotribal disfiguration fashion trends of today's disenfranchised youth. The author points out there is no reason to fear the unstructured nihilism from the Punks we encounter. *1997, 5½ x 8½, 112 pp, several photographs, soft cover.* **Order Number 94283. $8.95.**

FREEDOM ROAD
by Harold Hough

Have you dreamed about leaving the rat race but don't know where to start? This book will show you how to make a plan, eliminate your debts, and buy an RV. You'll learn about beautiful places where you can live for free. You'll learn how to make all the money you'll need from your hobbies. And you'll learn how to live a comfortable, healthy lifestyle on just a few dollars a day. Do the things you've been putting off: spending time with family, getting healthy, and being free! Why wait for retirement when you can live a low-cost, high travel lifestyle today? *1991, 5½ x 8½, 174 pp, illustrated, soft cover.* **Order Number 17056. $16.95.**

HOW TO START YOUR OWN COUNTRY
Second Edition
by Erwin S. Strauss

Start your own country? Yes! Thhis book tells the story of dozens of new country projects and explains the options available to those who want to start a country of their own. This daring approach to freedom has actually been tried many times in recent years, with varying degrees of success. Covers diplomacy, national defense, sovereignty, raising funds, recruiting settlers, and more, including names and addresses of current projects. Over 100 pages of fascinating case histories illustrated with dozens of rare photos. *1984, 5½ x 8½, 174 pp, illustrated, soft cover.* **Order Number 17028. $12.95.**

Travel-Trailer Homesteading Under $5,000
Second Edition
by Brian Kelling

Tired of paying rent? Need privacy away from nosy neighbors? This updated book will show how a modest financial investment can enable you to place a travel-trailer or other RV on a suitable piece of land and make the necessary improvements for a comfortable home in which to live! This book covers the cost break-down, tools needed, how to select the land and travel-trailer or RV, and how to install a septic system, as well as water, power (including solar panels), heat and refrigeration systems. This new edition covers how to cheaply install and run a hot tub, and reasons why you'll never want to leave your independence. *1999, 5½ x 8½, 112 pp, illustrated, soft cover.* **Order Number 14205. $10.00.**

SURVIVAL BARTERING
by Duncan Long

What if you had no money? What if an entire society had no money due to the collapse of our banking system? Bartering will be the most important survival skill you can learn. People barter for different reasons — to avoid taxes, obtain a better lifestyle, or just for fun. This book foresees a time when barter is a necessity. You'll learn about: three forms of bartaer; getting good deals; stockpiling for future bartering; protecting yourself from rip-offs; and much more. Learning how to barter could be the best insurance you can find. *1986, 5½ x 8½, 56 pp, soft cover.* **Order Number 13063. $8.00.**

THE LAST FRONTIERS ON EARTH
Strange Places Where You Can Live Free
by Jon Fisher

If you think there are no more frontiers on earth — if you think governments have got the territory sewed up — if you think there is nowhere you can go to be free of taxes, regulations, and restrictions — read this book. The Last Frontiers on Earth discusses living in Antarctica, on floating icebergs, onplatforms in the ocean, underwater, as a nomad, in an airship, and muchmore. For each place, the author considers cost of living, the availability of food and shelter, the climate and other important factors. There are places where you can live free — if you're determined. *1985, 5½ x 8½, 136 pp, illustrated, soft cover.* **Order Number 17032. $10.95.**

HOW TO LIVE WITHOUT ELECTRICITY — AND LIKE IT
by Anita Evangelista

There's no need to remain dependent on commercial electrical systems for your home's comforts and security. This book describes many alternative methods that can help you become more self-reliant and free from the utility companies. Leearn how to light, heat and cool your home, obtain and store water, cook and refrigerate food, and fulfill many other household needs without paying the power company! This book contains photographs, illustrations, and mail-order listings to make your transition to independence a snap! *1997, 5½ x 8½, 168 pp, illustrated, soft cover.* Order Number 14187. $13.95.

GETTING STARTED IN THE UNDERGROUND ECONOMY
by Adam Cash

Every year, billions of dollars go unreproted and untaxed in the underground economy — and, contrary to government propaganda, it's not all drug dealers and criminals, but ordinary Americans like yourself that have chosen to not report all or part of their income — to evade the excessive taxes the government keeps levying. This exciting book tells you how to join them! Don't believe the propaganda you hear about tax "cuts" — whatever the federal government cuts in taxes, it will make up inflation and new taxes. Adam Cash tells you how to ease your way into the tax-free imderground economy. *Sold for informational purposes only. 1987, 5½ x 8½, 160 pp, illustrated, soft cover.* Order Number 13068. $14.95.

GUERRILLA CAPITALISM
How to Practice Free Enterprise in an Unfree Economy
by Adam Cash

Guerrilla capitalists are people who practice free enterprise in the unfree economy. What good is "believing in" free enterprise if you don't practice it? This book gives you step-by-step instructions on how to do business "off the books;" doing busines without a license; getting customers to pay in cash; keeping two sets of books; investing unreported income; and much more. Highlighted with case histories of successful guerrilla capitalists, this book details the ins and outs of making money in the underground economy — without getting caught! 1984, 5½ x 8½, 172 pp, illustrated, soft cover. Order Number 13044. $146.95.

HOW TO DO BUSINESS "OFF THE BOOKS"
by Adam Cash

In Guerrilla Capitalism, Adam Cash showed you exactly how millions of Americans are defending themselves against a greedy government by evading taxes. No he digs even deeper into the secrets of the underground economy with this amazing book. The IRS contines its abuses of the rights of Americans, and governments at all levels continue to raise taxes and spend beyond their means. Americans at all levels are feeling the squeeze and are fighting back. Learn to keep your underground income "off the books" and deal with the IRS and others who want to burden you with taxes, fees, licensing requirements, etc. *1986, 5½ x 8½, 156 pp, soft cover.* Order Number 13056. $14.95.

SCRAM
Relocating Under a New Identity
by James S. Martin, Attorney at Law

Have you ever watched a ship go out to sea and wished you were on it, leaving your problems behind? You're not alone. Many people would love to make a fresh start, in a new town, under a new name. But how? This book will answer all your questions about relocating under a new identity. Covers: divorce; bankruptcy; ID; insurance; travel; your chances for success; and much more. Also included are ten real-life case histories that show problems and opportunities for identity-changers. *1993, 5½ x 8½, 83 pp, soft cover.* **Order Number 61138. $12.95.**

STREET SMARTS FOR THE NEW MILLINNEUM
by Jack Luger

Life can be risky for the average citizen. There are criminal elements in our society, as well as pitfalls in our everyday life, which pose real dangaers to the safety and security of ourselves and our families. In this unique book, author Jack Luger has provided the methods and resources that enable the reader to minimize the threats to our lives, liberties, and pursuit of happiness. You'll learn to: depend on personal resources instead of police; protect yourself, your family and your assets; and earn untraceable income. So don't be a victim! Learn to be self reliant, and arm yourself with the knowledge that it takes to develop your street smarts and survive this dangerous decade! *1996, 5½ x 8½, 138 pp, soft cover.* **Order Number 19197. $15.00.**

**You can get these books at your favorite bookstore
or contact any of our distributors:**

Bookpeople
7900 Edgewater Driver
Oakland, CA 94261
1-800-999-4650

Homestead Books
6101 22nd Avenue NW
Seattle, WA 98107
1-800-426-6777

Ingram Book Company
One Ingram Boulevard
La Vergne, TN 37086-1986
1-800-937-8000

Last Gasp of San Francisco
777 Florida Street
San Francisco, CA 94110
1-415-824-6636

Loompanics Unlimited
PO Box 1197
Port Townsend, WA 98368
1-800-380-2230